Antitrust, Competition Policy & State Professional Regulation:

A MANUAL FOR REGULATORS

The National Clearinghouse
on
Licensure, Enforcement and Regulation

The Council of State Governments
Lexington, Kentucky

Manufactured in the United States of America

EDITOR
Kim A. Zeitlin
Attorney at Law
Washington, D.C.

CONTRIBUTING EDITOR
Linda Jones
Attorney at Law
Baltimore, Maryland

CONTRIBUTORS
Charles Brown
Attorney General
West Virginia

Thomas McMahon
Chief, Anti-Trust Division
Colorado Department of Law

David Crump
Deputy Attorney General
North Carolina Department of Justice

Charles Monk
Deputy Attorney General
State of Maryland

William Dusso
Administrator
Wisconsin Department of Regulation and Licensing

Barbara Nichols
Secretary
Wisconsin Department of Regulation and Licensing

Anne Sawyer
University of North Carolina
Chapel Hill

Price: $15.00
C-32
ISBN-0-87292-059-3

Contents

Preface

When the United States Supreme Court in 1983 agreed to review the potential liability of several state board members in *Hoover v. Ronwin*, the antitrust exposure of state boards and board members received national attention. Since then, the National Clearinghouse on Licensure, Enforcement and Regulation (CLEAR) has developed this *Manual* to help state occupational and professional regulators understand this important area of state and federal law. The *Manual* is one of a series of educational manuals and reports CLEAR and The Council of State Governments have published since 1980.

Caroline Stellmann, Executive Director, Maryland Consumer Council, initiated development of the project, and Kim Zeitlin, Attorney, Washington, D.C., has served as chief editor for the Manual. Contributions were made by Charles Brown, Attorney General, West Virginia; David Crump, Deputy Attorney General, North Carolina Department of Justice; William Dusso, Administrator, Wisconsin Department of Regulation and Licensing; Linda Jones, Attorney, Baltimore, Maryland (formerly with the Maryland Department of Law); Thomas McMahon, Chief, Anti-Trust Unit, Colorado Department of Law; Charles Monk, Deputy Attorney General, Maryland Department of Law; Barbara Nichols, Secretary, Wisconsin Department of Regulation and Licensing; and Anne Sawyer, University of North Carolina.

CLEAR wishes to express its special recognition and appreciation to Kim A. Zeitlin, who served as editor-in-chief. Kim exercised leadership and provided considerable assistance throughout the project in working with the contributors and commenters in developing, researching, and revising the text and appendices. Linda Jones assisted Kim and CLEAR during this process.

Fran Berry, Director of CLEAR, guided the project throughout each phase.

We hope the *Manual* will be a valuable resource to the occupational and professional licensure officials in each state.

Carl W. Stenberg
Executive Director
The Council of State Government

Wellington Webb
Chairman, CLEAR and Executive Director
Colorado Department of Regulatory Agencies
August 1985

Introduction

States have a long-recognized interest in regulating a wide variety of occupations in order to protect their citizens. In general, a state may regulate an occupation where a rational connection exists between the regulation and the health, safety and welfare of the public. This principle, however, is subject to two qualifications. First, the regulating activity must be consistent with *constitutional* law such as the First Amendment, equal protection and due process. Second, the regulating activity must ordinarily also comply with any applicable federal or state *antitrust law*.

Since 1943 when the Supreme Court decided the case of *Parker v. Brown* and recognized for the first time that states themselves could be exempt from the federal antitrust laws by virtue of their status as sovereign powers, it had been assumed by some that all state agencies, including occupational licensing boards, enjoyed the same exemption as the state. However, the landmark *Goldfarb* case in 1975 and its progeny have made it clear that occupational licensing boards (and their members) may no longer assume that their actions are automatically shielded from antitrust exposure.

In recent years, the courts have found a variety of restrictive state economic initiatives to violate these principles. During 1985, the Federal Trade Commission was reported to be conducting at least 40 investigations of state boards in the health and other professions. Since the antitrust laws can also provide for treble damage remedies, and state boards and members have been sued privately and by the federal government, anticompetitive state regulation is an area of significant concern for board members, legislators, governors, attorneys general, their staffs, licensed and nonlicensed professionals, and the public.

The antitrust laws are state and federal laws which encourage competition and prohibit practices that unreasonably restrain that competition. The underlying premise is that the market place should generally determine the allocation of rewards in response to truthful competing offers of quality, service and price. Constraints on the free operations of the market are suspect and typically require justification. Since state regulation restricts the circumstances under which competition can occur, it can carry significant antitrust implications. This is especially sensitive where a state makes economic choices for its people which are not required by public health, safety or welfare. To address increased concern by providers and the public over the resolution of competition issues for professional services—especially in areas relating to professional competence—CLEAR and The Council of State Governments requested members of the regulatory community to develop this *Manual*.

In doing so, we identified several objectives. From the outset, we felt that the *Manual* should be different from current material. The *Manual* has been designed to satisfy the need of each lay state regulator for information—to be appraised in nontechnical terms of issues likely to be of direct concern. For this reason, the *Manual* focuses on several major doctrines. Our objective is to convey the concept and tone of these significant principles, both in current form and with an indication of potential areas of development.

We have decided to illustrate these points using federal law in particular because it reflects common themes in both federal and state regulation, it is more developed in the case literature than state antitrust law, it reflects a governmental perspective, and it is of great significance due to the influence of federal constitutional and statutory provisions on the activities of states. The reasons why federal antitrust law is important to state regulators are explored in further detail in the *Manual*.

The *Manual* illustrates some principles by using litigated decisions. Our emphasis is not primarily on defense against the possibility of litigation (although that is important) but on the areas of state regulation that bear most heavily on each regulator's day-to-day decisions in approaching competition issues that involve professional services. We place further emphasis on the quality, objectivity and thoroughness of these daily procedures and decisions. The *Manual* also differs from current material in that we have emphasized court cases and have included appendices focusing on occupational licensure and professional regulation in order to highlight the antitrust and competition principles.

In brief, the *Manual* is organized as follows. Chapter One describes the basic principles of antitrust law and policy which can influence board action. Chapter Two explores the immunity issue involving actions by the state (with an accompanying note on the separate "business of insurance" exemption). Chapter Three reviews immunity for petitioning the government. Chapter Four describes the importance of due process, equal protection and rational basis for decision making, and provides several specific examples of their application. Chapter Five concludes with observations based on the foregoing discussions.

As supportive matter, we have included footnotes and citations and have added seven appendices for more detailed reference. These appendices are: (I) a compilation of specific state antitrust statutes and constitutional provisions; (II) the text of pertinent federal antitrust laws which serve as models for considerable state legislation; (III) a statement of the six federal enforcement actions taken against state boards; (IV) a list of antitrust actions taken by the Department of Justice which involve the professions generally; (V) a list of selected antitrust actions taken by the Federal Trade Commission in the health care field; (VI) a sample state agency antitrust review provided with the assistance of Charles Monk and Michael Brockmeyer of the Office of the Maryland Attorney General; and (VII) a compendium of selected state antitrust authorities and opinions of state attorneys general on competition issues. We appreciate the comments and assistance of Arthur Lerner and Judith Moreland of the Bureau of Competition of the Federal Trade Commission in commenting on the text and assisting in the compilation of Appendix V. We hope these appendices will add to the interest and usefulness of the *Manual*.

The *Manual* discusses each subject in terms of a general problem, the doctrines that generally address the problem and the governmental, public and private concerns as well as exceptions. The *Manual* is a distillation of drafts and supplementary material provided by the contributors and editors. The Council of State Governments, and the contributors, commenters and editors do not advocate and take no position in the *Manual* with respect to any regulatory issues described, and the *Manual* does not necessarily represent their individual views. The *Manual* neither approves or disapproves the case authority.

The *Manual* is not a complete list or general explanation of the antitrust law. It is not legal advice, but is designed to provide state regulators of occupations with background to help them identify competition issues, analyze them with thoroughness and seek appropriate advice when necessary.

A state's competition policy is the body of rules and practices which establishes the basis on which professionals can lawfully offer their services to the public. Many boards and legislatures are re-examining the regulatory rules that govern the licensure and discipline process. We hope the *Manual* will encourage discussion and assist you with your work in developing and implementing your state's competition policy for professional services.

The editors and contributors extend to Fran Berry, Caroline Stellmann and the CLEAR Steering Committee our appreciation for their assistance in the development of the *Manual*. In particular, we enjoyed the collegial spirit which we had the opportunity to share during its preparation.

Kim A. Zeitlin
Editor

CHAPTER ONE
Antitrust and Competition Policy in State Professional Regulation: The Merits

In this chapter, we will review the historical background of the antitrust laws, their basic provisions, the two types of antitrust violations and several guidelines for analyzing issues of competition. The chapter will provide examples of some of the types of regulations which can raise issues of state competition policy and the impact of antitrust laws and the First Amendment on these questions. The chapter will also suggest practical ways in which you can analyze competition issues for professional services in your state.

Historical Background

The turn of the century ushered in a period of unprecedented vigor and growth in American industry, finance, agriculture and transportation. This growth transformed the American economy from one of relatively small competitive producers into one occasionally dominated and abused by various anticompetitive private economic combinations and trusts. These abuses of economic power—with resulting price increases and deterioration of quality—became the subject of daily press attention and led to the enactment of the Sherman Act[1] in 1890, the Clayton Act[2] in 1914 and the Federal Trade Commission Act[3] in the same year.

Application of the antitrust laws to the professions began in 1943, when the Supreme Court held in *American Medical Association v. United States*,[4] that the American Medical Association and the District of Columbia Medical Society had violated the criminal provisions of the Sherman Act by engaging in a conspiracy to obstruct the operation of a group health plan because it operated on a pre-paid rather than a fee-for-service basis. In 1975, the Supreme Court decided the landmark *Goldfarb* case, which held that a minimum fee schedule promulgated by a private bar association and enforced by the Virginia State Bar was a price fixing agreement under the antitrust law, and it was no defense that the practice of law was a "learned profession."[5] Since then the courts have assessed the legality under the antitrust laws of many other professional practices and their regulation by the states. In general the various professions subject to state licensing and regulation have been held to be in or affecting interstate commerce. Given the broad interpretation of the federal statutes many of their activities are likely to be subject to the federal acts.[6]

Several federal antitrust laws are most pertinent to state boards regulating the professions:

- Section 1 of the Sherman Act, 15 U.S.C. Section 1, prohibits contracts, combinations and conspiracies in unreasonable restraint of trade.
- Section 2 of the Sherman Act, 15 U.S.C. Section 2, prohibits monopolization and attempts and conspiracies to monopolize.
- Section 4 of the Clayton Act, 15 U.S.C. Section 15, provides for private actions and treble damages plus attorney's fees for violation of the antitrust laws. Injunctive relief is available for both the government and private parties.
- Section 5 of the Federal Trade Commission Act, 15 U.S.C. Section 45, prohibits unfair methods of competition and unfair or deceptive acts or practices and is enforced by the Federal Trade Commission without a private damage remedy. (See Appendix II for the full text of these sections.)

The states have similar antitrust statutes (See Appendix I) which are applicable to intra-state commerce not subject to the federal antitrust laws.

The Basic Tests of Legality

Antitrust violation ordinarily requires at least two entities to form an agreement whose purpose or effect is to restrain trade; unilateral action (except for monopolization) is not enough.[7] However, this rule does not apply in monopolization cases and its application is currently unclear in the cases of licensing and other standard-setting groups.

Per Se

Certain conduct is deemed so lacking in any competitive justification that it is regarded as automatically (*per se*) illegal. Examples of such behavior are agreements to fix prices, prohibit all competitive bidding, or to engage in certain boycotts and division of markets. In addition, a blanket prohibition on all advertising or on all solicitation of business may well fall into this category.[8]

Per se treatment is important for two reasons. First, where a *per se* violation is established, it is not necessary to show precise harm to competition caused by the general pernicious effect of the practice on competition. Second, the federal antitrust agencies are especially interested in *per se* behavior sanctioned by state boards. *Every* federal enforcement action initiated thus far against state boards has alleged either established *per se* violations or alleged advertising and solicitation restraints which may fall into this category. (See Appendix III.)

Rule of Reason

Other types of restraints are tested by the "Rule of Reason" described by Justice Brandeis in *Chicago Board of Trade v. United States*:[9]

> The true test of legality [under the Rule of Reason] is whether the restraint imposed in such as merely regulates and perhaps thereby *promotes competition or* whether it is such as may *suppress or even destroy competition.* To determine that question the court must ordinarily consider the facts peculiar to the business to which the restraint is applied; its condition before and after the restraint was imposed; the nature of the restraint and its effect, actual or probable. The history of the restraint, the evil believed to exist, the reason for adopting the particular remedy, the purpose or end sought to be attained, are all relevant facts. (italics added.)

Competition is firmly established as national policy under the antitrust laws, and it is no defense that competition itself is unreasonable or bad. Considerations unrelated to the effect of the restraints on competition are generally not relevant.

For example, The Rule of Reason did not permit an association of competing engineers to justify its total ban on competitive bidding on the contention that buildings would fall down if engineers engaged in competition in their bidding.

Genuine professional ethical principles (not commercial restraints) are also susceptible to Rule of Reason analysis because they may promote competition. These genuine professional ethical standards include prohibitions against conflicts of interest and legitimate professional discipline of incompetent practitioners. As stated by the Supreme Court: "[E]thical norms may serve to regulate and promote this competition, and thus fall within the Rule of Reason."[10] Although the precise parameters are not yet clear, restraints in the health field which are *pro*-competitive may be lawful under the Rule of Reason. The courts have also considered whether the alleged restraint promotes a valid (not speculative) patient health care interest, whether it is secondary (ancillary) to a lawful main purpose, or whether it is used in a manner which is not unduly restrictive of competition (such as reasonable and valid rules for determining professional competence). If so, the Rule of Reason may be satisfied.[11]

First Amendment-Related Issues

The First Amendment's guarantee of free speech is a principle of constitutional law and not antitrust law. However, because of the close relationship (such as between advertising and competition), the principles underlying the First Amendment are receiving increased attention as a basis for *per se* and Rule of Reason antitrust treatment.

Professionals have a constitutional right to speak and consumers have a constitutional right to hear truthful (not false, misleading, deceptive or illegal) advertising and other commercial information. Therefore, truthful advertising of price or availability of professional services generally cannot be restrained by the state.[12] However, where deception has occurred or is likely, restraints narrowly drawn to solve the problem have been permitted, as in the case of the likelihood of undue influence presented by in-person professional solicitation or a prior history of deception in a state surrounding the use of trade names.[13]

Analysis of Potential *Per Se* or Rule-of-Reason Issues

A court's choice to use either the *per se* or Rule of Reason analysis is important, for *per se* analysis excludes complicated economic proof. Regulators should be particularly mindful of two points:

1. Restraints upon practice, competitive bidding, advertising and solicitation are subject to possible *per se* or First Amendment treatment and should be approached with the greatest care.

2.Regardless of whether *per se* or Rule of Reason antitrust analysis would be applied by a court or administrative agency, any proposed regulation that imposes a potential competitive disadvantage to any group or individual should be accompanied by due process. This includes a record that reviews and substantiates the purpose and effect of the regulation. In occupational licensure, the record should carefully examine and substantiate whether proposals promote the public interest in making choices available among competent practitioners.

Despite their importance, the detailed nuances of a health and safety antitrust defense in a litigation are not the principal concern of board members during a rulemaking. Before embarking upon the regulatory program, a board must be satisfied that it has the authority to act in the manner contemplated. Once this concern is met,the board is responsible to obtain and determine facts and formulate judgments based on a full record.[14] In addition to the factors mentioned in the *Chicago Board of Trade* decision, the following questions may assist your board in determining a proper response to proposals carrying potential anticompetitive consequences:

- Who is proposing the regulation?
- Have you insured that all interested groups have had notice of the proposal and an opportunity to comment and otherwise make a due process record?
- Is the proposal substantiated by scientific or other facts?
- Is the justification offered consistent with the terms, breadth and likely effect of the proposal?
- Is the proposal supported by disinterested tes-

timony? Do consumers support the proposal? Who will be helped or hurt by the proposal?

- What is the relevant experience in other states if any?
- Is the situation at issue adequately addressed by the market and does the proposal offer the least restrictive available alternative? Does the proposal offer consumers choices among competent personnel?
- Does the proposal in fact promote competent use of skills and provide for sanctions against incompetent practice?
- If you are not satisfied with the record, have you sought additional record information? Have you considered seeking disinterested expert testimony where disputed technical issues are involved?
- Is this proposal necessary? Are you persuaded on a factual record that it is a good idea?

Each state must determine its own policies, but these questions may supplement your own inquiry in developing your state's competition policy in the field of professional services.

Examples

As illustrations, several types of board regulations can raise competition *issues*. Under the antitrust principles discussed above, some of these regulations may be sustainable

Price-Related Activity.

Price-fixing exists when two or more competitors conspire or agree to fix, raise, lower, stabilize or in any way affect the price to be charged for a product or service. This is the classic *per se* violation. In occupational licensing, a regulation setting forth a fee schedule or requiring compliance with a fee schedule adopted by a trade association are regulations which may raise price-fixing issues. Other regulations raising price issues are ones which:

- Prohibit a licensee from working for a salary or requiring that the licensee be compensated on a fee-for-service basis.
- Prohibit fee advertising or free services.
- Restrict competition on the basis of design, price or competitive bidding.
- Require compliance with relative-value scales or which provide information permitting the relative-value scale to be used as a fee schedule.

Advertising and Solicitation.

As previously noted, the states may not ordinarily restrain truthful commercial speech. Two current issues of interest, however, are the permissible limits of solicitation of business and whether and how a professional may be required to substantiate advertising claims. Both may turn on the requirement that state regulation not chill First Amendment expression. Advertising and solicitation restraints—whether under the antitrust laws or the First Amendment—remain a highly sensitive area.

Restrictions on Entry.

Occupational standards that distinguish between candidates on the basis of valid measures of competence are lawful under the Rule of Reason. However, occupational standards for obtaining a license that have no reasonable relationship to competency or protection of the public health, safety and welfare may be anticompetitive. These include discriminatory entry standards such as those based on age, residency, citizenship, or membership in trade associations. In addition, reciprocity rules that establish stricter qualifications for persons licensed in other jurisdictions may raise competition issues.[15]

Form and Conduct of Business.

Restrictions in this category prohibit a professional from conducting his or her occupation in a certain commercial manner. They could include restrictions which prohibit:

- Opening of a branch or satellite office.
- Practice in a shopping center or other commercial establishment.
- Establishing a practice or other professional relationship with practitioners of other occupations. For example, lawyers traditionally have been prohibited from entering into a partnership with accountants to provide both legal and accounting services to the public.
- Employment by a business entity that has officers and directors who are not members of the same occupation.
- Practicing under a trade name.
- Use of a form of business organization not historically recognized in the profession, such as an organization of medical or legal practices, as corporations rather than as partnerships.
- Work or reimbursement other than under the supervision of or with the approval of another professional. An example is a rule requiring a physician or other health care provider to obtain the "consent" of a patient's former physician before commencing treatment.

Method of Practice

- Restrictions on the use of professionals to perform procedures that they are competent to perform. This issue arises frequently in the health care area where there have traditionally been significant restrictions on practice by physician's assistants and various types of nurses. A variant of this could be an arbitrary requirement of "direct supervision" or an arbitrary numerical "staffing ratio."
- Unreasonable inhibitions on innovation in practice. This could include regulations that prohibit members of the occupation from using procedures that are safe, efficacious and that have scientific validity but which are not recognized by a leading trade association or a particular certifying agency.

Conclusion

This chapter has summarized several basic antitrust principles applicable when analyzing issues relating to the regulation of professions. Since each state has a different set of priorities and circumstances, no one set of questions can be used for every state. Nevertheless, certain goals apply to all. With the basic principles outlined, you as a regulator can evaluate the options open to you as well as any risks involved in making choices for professional regulation in your state.

Notes

1. 15 U.S.C. Section 1 *et seq.*
2. 15 U.S.C. Section 12 *et seq.*
3. 15 U.S.C. Section 41 *et seq.*
4. 317 U.S. 519 (1943).
5. Goldfarb v. Virginia State Bar, 421 U.S. 773 (1975).
6. *See, e.g.*, cases collected in Marrese v. Interqual, Inc., 748 F.2d 373 (7th Cir. 1984).
7. *E.g.*, United States v. Colgate & Co., 250 U.S. 300 (1919).
8. *E.g.*, Arizona v. Maricopa County Medical Society, 457 U.S. 332 (1982) (price-fixing); National Society of Professional Engineers v. United States, 435 U.S. 679 (1978) (competitive bidding).
9. 24 U.S. 231, 238 (1918), *cited in* National Society of Professional Engineers v. United States, *supra*, 435 U.S. at 691; *see* Northwest Wholesale Stationers, Inc. v. Pacific Stationery and Printing Co., 53 U.S.L.W. 4733 (1985) and cases cited therein.
10. National Society of Professional Engineers v. United States, *supra*, 435 U.S. at 696.
11. *See* American Society of Mechanical Engineers, Inc. v. Hydrolevel Corp., 456 U.S. 556, 577 (1982); Indiana Federation of Dentists v. Federal Trade Commission, 745 F.2d 1124 (7th Cir. 1984), *petition for cert. filed*, No. 84-1809 (U.S. May 17, 1985); Kreuzer v. American Academy of Periodontology, 735 F.2d 1479 (D.C. Cir. 1984); Weiss v. York Hospital, 745 F.2d 786 (3rd Cir. 1984), *cert. denied,* 105 S. Ct. 1777 (1985); Wilk v. American Medical Association, 719 F.2d 207, 227 (7th Cir. 1983), *cert. denied*, 104 S.Ct.2398 (1984); Ratino v. Medical Service of the District of Columbia, 718 F.2d 1260 (4th Cir. 1983); Hospital Building Co. v. Trustees of Rex Hospital, 691 F.2d 678 (4th Cir. 1982), *cert. denied*, 104 S.Ct. 231, 259 (1983); Feminist Women's Health Center, Inc. v. Mohammad, 586 F.2d 530 (5th Cir. 1978), *cert. denied*, 444 U.S. 924 (1979); *cf.* Arizona v. Maricopa County Medical Society, *supra*, 457 U.S. at 348-49 (1982).
12. Zauderer v. Office of Disciplinary Counsel, 53 U.S.L.W. 4587 (1985); In re RMJ, 455 U.S. 191, 203 (1982); Village of Hoffman Estates v. Flipside Hoffman Estates, Inc., 455 U.S. 489 (1982); Bates v. State Bar of Arizona, 433 U.S. 350 (1977); In re Primus, 436 U.S. 412 (1978); Virginia Pharmacy Board v. Virginia Citizens Consumer Council, 425 U.S. 748 (1976); *cf.* Bolger v. Youngs Drug Products Corp., 463 U.S. 60 (1983); American Medical Association, 94 F.T.C. 701 (1979), *aff'd sub nom.* American Medical Association v. F.T.C., 638 F.2d 443 (2d Cir. 1980), *aff'd per curiam by an equally divided court*, 455 U.S. 676 (1982).
13. *See* Ohralik v. Ohio State Bar Ass'n, 436 U.S. 447 (1978) (possibility of "fraud, undue influence, intimidation, overreaching"; limitations on in-person solicitation by lawyers); Friedman v. Rogers, 440 U.S. 1 (1979) (history of deception in Texas supports prohibition by Texas on use of trade names by optometrists).
14. *Cf., e.g.,* Motor Vehicle Manufacturers Assocation v. State Farm Mutual, 463 U.S. 29 (1983).
15. *See* Supreme Court of New Hampshire v. Piper, 105 S.Ct. 1272 (1985) (residency); Bogus v. American Speech & Hearing Association, 582 F.2d 277 (3rd Cir. 1978) (membership).

CHAPTER TWO

Immunity by Action of the State

In *Hoover v. Ronwin*[1], a state bar admissions committee and its members were held to be a committee of the sovereign state supreme court and were immune from antitrust suit. Therefore you might ask: if state boards and committees can be immune from suit, what is the concern for antitrust exposure for our board? A partial answer is that immunity is not uniform. This chapter will examine the circumstances under which you and your board may be immune—and where exposure is most likely. Lack of immunity may not only result in injunctive relief to overturn your board's work, but can potentially subject you and your board to treble-damage exposure. In some instances, your immunity may depend on interpretation of your state's statutes and the degree of anticompetitive conduct which you require. The subject of immunity is therefore of concern not only to boards, but board members, staff, and professional associations which have an interest in board work. Statutes, regulations, and their policies and interpretations are the day-to-day work of regulators and therefore we will examine several statutory-regulatory schemes in this chapter.

The State Action Doctrine

Under our constitutional system, the actions of sovereign states are respected. In general terms, the federal antitrust laws are interpreted as not applying to policy actions of sovereign states—a doctrine known as the "state action" doctrine. If the doctrine applies (as discussed further in this chapter), the state and certain *private* parties may ordinarily engage in anticompetitive activity immune from the antitrust laws.[2] The general issue is the *degree* of state involvement. Accordingly, the simple contention that an occupation is a "state-regulated profession," without more, is an insufficient degree of state involvement to demonstrate that the state has acted to confer antitrust immunity on a licensing board. Anticompetitive conduct, by itself, neither creates nor withdraws immunity; the question is whether an anticompetitive policy is actually your state's policy and the degree of your state's involvement in and supervision of that policy.[3]

For immunity purposes, the sovereign power of the state can be exercised by the judicial and legislative branches and possibly the executive branch as well. At one end of the spectrum, a licensing board that is part and parcel of a sovereign state supreme court has been held immune from the antitrust challenge that an examination cut-off score was used to exclude candidates for anticompetitive purposes.[4] On the other end of the spectrum, a state board that is not closely tied to its sovereign legislature and whose prohibitions against competitive bidding were not legislative policy was held not immune.[5] In each case, the degree of state involvement in an anticompetitive policy was considered.

The State Itself

Of particular concern to legislatively created or authorized boards (whether autonomous or not) are situations where the legislature acts as sovereign. The doctrine of state action immunity was recognized in *Parker v. Brown*[6] in in which a California statute established a system to regulate the production and marketing of California raisins. The program was implemented by an advisory commission including the state director of agriculture. The purpose of the statute was to protect producers by restricting competition among growers and to maintain prices in the distribution to packers. The U.S. Supreme Court found the existence of "state action or official action directed by a state."[7] In *Parker*, the Court held that "nothing in the language of the Sherman Act or in its history . . . suggests that its purpose was to restrain a state or its officers or agents from activities *directed by its legislature*." (italics added)[8] The decision emphasized the state legislature's decision; the mere participaton of private producers in the marketing system did not detract from the state character of the program.

Concerning another action of the legislature as sovereign, in *New Motor Vehicle Board of California v. Orrin W. Fox*,[9] a statute required automobile manufacturers to advise existing franchisees of the manufacturer's desire to relocate or establish another retail dealer in the existing area. This allowed existing businesses to prevent introduction of a competitor by filing a protest with a state board, which would then hear and determine the competitive effects of the proposal and decide whether the new dealer would be permitted to open.

The U.S. Supreme Court held that the statute identified a "clearly articulated and affirmatively expressed" state policy and system to "displace unfettered business freedom in the matter of the establishment and relocation of automobile dealerships."[10] The state board's hearings were also viewed as active supervision of the state's policy. The Supreme Court thus concluded that the state had acted, and held the anticompetitive program immune from federal antitrust suit.

Similarly, in *Bates v. State Bar of Arizona,*[11] a

ban on professional advertising was held immune from antitrust challenge because the action was taken primarily by and through the sovereign state supreme court, with private associations acting as an agent and under the continuing supervision of the sovereign. However, as discussed in Chapter One, the advertising restraint was invalidated on First Amendment grounds.

In each of these Supreme Court decisions, the court found immunity from federal antitrust law where the state acted as the sovereign. However, other cases have reached *different* conclusions when they involve essentially *private* anticompetitive conduct (and not that of the state) if there was either no clear state policy to displace competition or no active supervision of private conduct. Some of the court analysis of statutes and regulations is detailed and somewhat technical, but as we review these cases you will see further the critical role which your statutes, regulations and supervision play in determining immunity of boards and board members while establishing state competition policy in professional services.

In *Goldfarb v. Virginia State Bar,*[12] a county wide fee schedule for lawyers was attacked as an illegal price fixing agreement. The conduct was held not to be that of the state. Nothing in Virginia law required or authorized the minimum fees by private bar associations. The U.S. Supreme Court rejected the claim that immunity was required because law is a state-regulated profession and private price fixing by minimum fees "complemented" state regulation of lawyers. If price fixing for professional services was not state policy (and it was not), there was no basis to immunize the price fixing in *Goldfarb*.

In *Cantor v. Detroit Edison Co.*[13] a state statute provided for general electric utility regulation in Michigan. A regulated utility decided to give away free light bulbs to stimulate its business and included reference to this program in the tariffs filed with and approved by the state public utility commission. However, a seller of light bulbs challenged the utility's give-away program claiming that the program restrained his trade. The utility claimed that approval of the tariff by the State's public utility commission created state action immunity. The Supreme Court held that the program was *not* immune because neither the Michigan legislature nor the public utility commission had actively considered or passed upon any competitive issues raised by the program. The mere filing and general approval of that utility's tariff by the commission was a neutral act and not the articulation of an *active state policy* to displace competition. There was simply no state competition *policy* regarding distribution of free light bulbs. With no state competition policy on light bulbs, the court had no basis for finding immunity.

The leading case of *California Retail Liquor Dealers Association v. Midcal Aluminum, Inc. (Midcal)*[14] further illustrates this analysis. There a state statute authorized private price setting and private enforcement of California's wholesale wine resale pricing. However, the state did not actively supervise this program. It did not, for example, establish or review the prices, regulate the terms of the resale contract, monitor market conditions, conduct "pointed re-examination of the program," and generally did not "completely control" wine distribution through "comprehensive regulation" so as to "displace business freedom with its [the state's] own power."[15] The court found no immunity.

To summarize these authorities:

- Conduct by the state itself acting in its sovereign capacity is generally immune regardless of the anticompetitive consequences.[16]
- Immunity is created if the tests in *Midcal* are met—clearly articulated and affirmatively expressed state policy to displace competition with either regulation or monopoly plus "active state supervision" of private conduct.

The *Ronwin* case determined that since the decision to admit attorneys was made by the sovereign state supreme court, those acting on its behalf were immune as part of the sovereign. However, in situations of much greater interest to many regulators—the exposure of *legislatively created* state regulatory boards—the U.S. Supreme Court expressly *reserved* judgment on the boards' antitrust exposure:

"The consequences of reversal by the Court today [upholding immunity] will have only a limited effect. Our attention has not been drawn to any trade or other profession in which the licensing of its members is determined directly by the sovereign itself—here the state Supreme Court."[17]

Turning to this area of more immediate concern—legislatively created or legislatively authorized boards—it should be noted that *Ronwin* also reserved the question of "whether the governor of a State stands in the same position as the legislature or the Supreme Court for purposes of the state action doctrine."[18] A recent lower court decision has expressed the view that certain executive functions are sovereign for this purpose.[19]

As we have seen, the general problem of state immunity concerns the relationship between the state statute and the specific anticompetitive board regulation.

The Midcal Tests

a. *Clear State Policy to Displace Competition*

Where a statute is explicit and anticompetitive (such as requiring that denturists receive work only from dentists and not patients), board regulation closely following the statute has been upheld.[20] However, where a statute does not direct a ban on competitive bidding, board regulation has been held to be not protected.[21]

Statutes are commonly not explicit as to potentially anticompetitive board regulation. In one such case, clear state policy has been found and immunity has been upheld where the conduct was a foreseeable result in carrying out the legislature's intent in establishing the regulatory scheme.

In the leading case of *Southern Motor Carriers Rate Conference v. United States,*[22] rate bureaus in North Carolina, Georgia, Tennessee and Mississippi submitted joint rate proposals to the public service commissions in each state. This collective ratemaking was authorized but not compelled by each state. The U.S. Supreme Court held that state *authorization* of joint ratemaking in that case was a sufficiently clear policy to displace competition with regulation.

Several comments may be helpful. First, the Court emphasized that the activity challenged (and *not* the identity of the defendant) was the issue. On the issue of how much specificity is necessary to establish a "clear" state policy, the Court found state intent to adopt a "permissive" policy which "permits a range of regulatory alternatives." The court rejected the argument that the anticompetitive act must be "necessary" or "compelled" by the legislature. In an important qualification, the Court ruled that "compulsion" is often the best evidence of the state's clearly articulated and affirmatively expressed policy to displace competition. Immunity can be found if compulsion is absent, and if "other evidence" does "conclusively" show 'that a state intends to adopt a permissive policy.[23] In *Southern Motor Carriers*, the Mississippi statute did not explicitly address joint rulemaking and thus did not compel the action. However, the state did establish, a regulatory structure to displace competition, the state public service commission actively encouraged joint ratemaking practice, and it was conceded that the state actively supervised the conduct of the private parties.

Southern Motor Carriers is a generally favorable decision for state boards and their members and is likely to have greater overall impact than the celebrated *Ronwin* case. *Southern Motor Carriers* establishes a framework to analyze acts of sovereign legislatures in connection with the activities of many regulatory boards and not just an examination committee acting as a part of a sovereign state supreme court which made actual decisions on candidates in *Ronwin*. The precise meaning of the Supreme Court's observation about "conclusive" evidence short of compulsion is still unclear. However the courts and the federal antitrust agencies will interpret *Southern Motor Carriers* in cases involving state boards,[24] and state boards and legislatures will draft legislation and regulations in response to this decision. Some boards have already begun this process.

In reviewing the questions of clear state policy and whether the legislature contemplated displacing competition, we can expect the courts to continue to look to factors such as to the regulatory scheme, state judicial decision, legislative history, recent legislative action and board interpretation.[25] However, a comprehensive statutory scheme will not necessarily provide immunity; statutes may protect some conduct but not all.[26] The effect on pre-*Southern Motor Carriers* case law is uncertain,[27] as is the question of whether a defendant will be required to demonstrate that immunity exists.[28] Where conduct falls outside the scope of board authority, the conduct will probably not be immune—either because it lacks the necessary clear state policy (as may arguably be the case with *per se*-type federal enforcement actions against boards brought before *Southern Motor Carriers*) or because it lacks the necessary active state supervision discussed below.[29]

Still, one prudent course for a practitioner-dominated board contemplating restrictive regulatory action (which may be viewed by some as *per se* illegal or blatantly anticompetitive) is to be confident that the board is acting under a state statute which is explicit on that point. To the extent there is such a statute, there can be little argument that state action exemption is applicable. To the extent there is not, there may be questions of whether the exemption is applicable, whether the interest of the public is being served by the board's proposed action, or whether a "public policy" identified by the board is arbitrary or speculative.

b. *Active Supervision*

In addition to the "clear state policy" ground discussed above, active supervision has been a requirement for finding immunity. For example, the *New Motor Vehicle* case discussed above illustrates the presence of active state supervision, while the decision in *Midcal* illustrates the absence of such supervision.

In *Town of Hallie v. City of Eau Claire,*[30] the U.S. Supreme Court held that where the conduct of a municipality is involved, there is no need for active supervision by the state. Since active supervision is merely to assure that the conduct comes under a state policy, the Court found that the municipality acted under articulated state policy which eliminated a necessity to show active supervision. The court noted that "in cases in which the actor is a state agency, it is likely that active state supervision would also not be required, although we do not here decide that issue."[31] However, the Court reaffirmed the requirement of "active state supervision" where "state or municipal regulation of a private party is involved."[32]

Several other cases further illustrate the meaning of "active supervision." In *Marrese v. Interqual, Inc.,*[33] the Court found that Indiana's comprehensive scheme and supervision of medical peer review (including the state medical board and hospital licensing council), which were legislatively mandated with members appointed by the governor, constituted active supervision and were therefore immune from an antitrust challenge to termination of a physician's hospital privileges. However, the Court's limited discussion of the authority of the state hospital licensing council, and the fact that the state medical board may not have been able to supervise any restraints imposed by the hospital peer review board, may raise questions under this analysis.

In *Miller v. Oregon Liquor Control Commission*,[34] the state mandated the posting of prices to be charged by each wholesaler. However, Oregon did not establish prices, review the reasonableness of posted price schedules, monitor market conditions or engage in any pointed re-examination of the program. Immunity was denied. Failure to actively supervise resale prices also resulted in denial of immunity in *JAJ Liquor Store v. New York State Liquor Authority*.[35]

Another case illustrating the need to show active supervision is *State of North Carolina v. P.I.A. Asheville, Inc.*[36] There the acquisition of a private psychiatric hospital by the largest operator of such hospitals was challenged under the antitrust laws. Although the Court found that the state action doctrine could apply because of the state's involvement in the certificate-of-need requirements for authorizing hospital beds, the state did not monitor the use of the hospital after acquisition, post-acquisition prices, penalities for failure to obtain certificate-of-need, or otherwise monitor conduct of health care providers there. The Court found what it described as a "total absence of supervision" after issuance of certificate-of-need and held no immunity. It is clear that active supervision will be a key area of court attention in future challenges—particularly to board-related private conduct.[37]

A Note on the "Business of Insurance" Exemption

As a final point on comprehensive state regulation, a limited separate exemption by statute exists for the "business of insurance" under the McCarran-Ferguson Act.[38] The act provides that the business of insurance shall be subject to state law; that no Act of Congress shall be construed to invalidate, impair, or supersede any state law regulating the business of insurance (unless such an act specifically relates to the business of insurance); that federal antitrust law applies to the extent insurance is not regulated by state law; and that nothing contained in the McCarran-Ferguson Act renders the Sherman Act inapplicable to any agreement to boycott, coerce, or intimidate, or any act of boycott, coercion, or intimidation. As noted in *Union Labor Life v. Pireno*,[39] the basic purpose of the act was to foster intra-industry cooperation on ratemaking necessary for underwriting insurance risk. Situations falling within the exemption include fixing of rates between insurer and insured; selling and advertising of policies; and licensing of companies and agents.[40]

However, the exemption is narrow. First, it does not apply to boycotts, and many situations fall outside the exemption for this reason.[41] Second, the courts have considered factors concerning the exemption as stated in *Pireno*:[42]

"First, whether the practice has the effect of transferring or spreading a policy-holder's risk; second, whether the practice is an integral part of the policy relationship between the insurer and the insured; and third, whether the practice is limited to entities within the insurance industry."

Thus even pervasive state regulation of insurance would not, by itself, be sufficient to qualify for exemption unless the nonboycott and *Pireno* requirements are also met.

Insurance has assumed increased significance in reimbursement, particularly for health-care personnel. The scope of coverage, reasonableness of rates, and minimization of delay or interference with claims evaluation and processing are subjects of daily concern to those requiring coverage and to employers, hospitals, providers, and potential providers. Insurance is often a price-related matter, but also relates to scope of practice, petitioning the government, and possibly state action. The antitrust problem is particularly acute where providers control insurers and are in a conflict of interest on controlling insurance costs.[43]

Regulators should carefully review proposed insurance arrangements in a manner similar to the need to review tariffs as discussed earlier in this chapter. The fact that an insurance company regulated by the state submits a proposal does not mean it is part of the "business of insurance." Rather, the board should determine the consequences of the proposal and make a judgment as to whether it is consistent with and promotes state competition policies.

Conclusion

Several general observations about state action may be pertinent. The state action issue is partly a question of whether a state wishes to engage in serious, systematic oversight of professionals. Specific legislation also helps licensure officials by providing guidance. Where the state mandate is unclear, board members should be cautious in imposing anticompetitive restraints. Ultimately, board members may wish to consider reviewing their legislation with its regulatory purpose and the foregoing discussion in Chapter One in mind.

The state action doctrine does not apply automatically. The Maryland attorney general has informed boards that his office may not defend boards if their conduct is anticompetitive and not required by the legislature. Boards avoid considerable difficulty by identifying antitrust problems in advance. The antitrust review illustrated in Appendix VI illustrates a method used in Maryland for obtaining this assistance. Boards which do not have the benefit of this type of antitrust review should consider available alternatives. Insurance or other protection to address the risk of asserting a state action defense, defense costs and any damage exposure can be considered. Although state officials are generally immune for acts taken in good faith within the scope of their authority,[44] this principle has not received extensive interpretation in the context of antitrust exposure of state board members. The principle may be inapplicable for intentional denials of due process with anticompetitive purpose or effect or conspiracies with private groups, or acts beyond an official's authority. For instance, in *Feminist Women's Health Center v. Mohammad*,[45] the president of the Florida State Board of Medical Examiners sent a letter on board letterhead urging other Florida physicians to boycott a physician offering favorable competitive terms. The president was held not immune from antitrust suit. In another case, the Iowa commissioner of health was also held not immune from suit on allegations he improperly participated in and furthered a conspiracy against chiropractors.[46] There is authority even before the *Goldfarb* case that recognized that *ultra vires* acts (beyond the power of state officials) are not immune from the antitrust laws.[47] In a contrasting trial court decision, the Oregon state director of workmen's compensation was held immune from allegations by chiropractors that he had acted with bias in denying reimbursement to chiropractors.[48] Appeal of this decision is pending. Much of this problem can be avoided by confining anticompetitive regulation to the explicit requirements of enabling legislation.

Autonomous boards are in an uncertain position under the state action doctrine even after the most recent decisions. Depending on their particular characteristics, they have elements of sovereign, nonsovereign representative, legislative, executive, private or mixed status—all of which remain to be analyzed in detail by the courts. The immunity results may well depend on the degree of state policy and supervision involvement in their activities. Another area of uncertainty for autonomous boards is the interrelationship between state action, which may delegate some public functions to private groups, and state constitutional law which can prohibit certain delegations.[49] Given the current uncertain and developing state of the law of immunity, boards are well-advised to approach anticompetitive proposals with care.

There is much litigation in this area and some recent decisions by the U.S. Supreme Court have upheld immunity of board members on the facts of those cases. However, it is not certain how these decisions will be interpreted in subsequent disputes, or how the facts of future cases will affect their outcomes. In general, boards should follow guides along the lines suggested in Chapter One when considering regulatory conduct which may have anticompetitive implications. The discussion in this chapter highlights the principle that the greater the potential for restricting competition, the greater the benefits of statutory authorization. Boards should be aware that in addition to the benefits of clear indication of state policy by statute, active state supervision has been required to qualify much board action for state action immunity.

The principle of active state supervision is not only a doctrine of antitrust law, however. It also reflects the fundamental importance of serious and responsible professional regulation in the public interest.

Notes

1. 104 S.Ct. 1989 (1984).
2. *Cf.* Rice v. Norman Williams, 458 U.S. 654 (1982).
3. *See* California Retail Liquor Dealer's Ass'n v. Midcal Aluminum, 445 U.S. 97 (1980).
4. Hoover v. Ronwin, 104 S.Ct. at 1991, n.1, *supra*.
5. United States v. Texas State Board of Public Accountancy, 464 F. Supp. 400 (W.D. Tex. 1978), *aff'd*, 592 F.2d 919 (5th Cir.), *cert. denied*, 444 U.S. 925 (1979).
6. 317 U.S. 341 (1943).
7. *Id.* at 350-351.
8. *Id.*
9. 439 U.S. 96 (1978).
10. *Id.* at 109.
11. 433 U.S. 350 (1977).
12. 421 U.S. 773 (1975).
13. 428 U.S. 579 (1976).
14. 445 U.S. 97 (1980).
15. *Id.* at 106.
16. *Cf.* note 3, *supra*. The Supreme Court applied *Midcal* to municipalities in Community Communications Co., Inc. v. City of Boulder, 455 U.S. 40 (1982). *But see* Town of Hallie v. City of Eau Claire, 105 S.Ct. 1713 (1985) (no requirement of active supervision for municipalities). Under the impetus of Senator Strom Thurmond, chairman of the Senate Judiciary Committee, Congress amended the federal antitrust laws by enacting the Local Government Antitrust Act of 1984, Pub.L. 544. This legislation provides substantial antitrust protection for municipalities and municipal officials, and is included in Appendix II of the *Manual*.
17. 104 S.Ct. at 2002, n.34.
18. 104 S.Ct. at 1995, n.17.
19. Deak-Perera Hawaii, Inc. v. Department of Transportation, State of Hawaii, 745 F.2d 1281 (9th Cir. 1984), *cert. denied*, 105 S.Ct. 1756-57 (1985).

20. See Gambrel v. Kentucky Board of Dentistry, 689 F.2d 612 (6th Cir. 1982), *cert. denied*. 459 U.S. 1208 (1983); Benson v. Arizona State Board of Dental Examiners, 673 F.2d 272 (9th Cir. 1982); *cf.* Brazil v. Arkansas Board of Dental Examiners, 593 F. Supp. 1354 (E.D. Ark. 1984).

21. United States v. Texas State Board of Public Accountancy, supra.

22. 105 S.Ct. at 1721 (1985).

23. 105 S.Ct. at 1729-30.

24. Cases against boards initiated before *Southern Motor Carriers* include: United States v. Mississippi State Board for Professional Engineers and Land Surveyors, 3 Trade Cas. (CCH) para. 45,080 (D.C. Miss. Civ. No. J-80-0235, 1980) (consent decree) (restraint on competitive bidding); United States v. Alaska Board of Registration for Architects, Engineers and Land Surveyors, 3 Trade Cas. (CCH) para.50,837 (D. Alaska 1983) (consent decree) (restraint on competitive bids and price quotation); United States v. Louisiana Board of Certified Public Accountants, Civ. No. 83-1947 (E.D.La.—filed April 15, 1983); FTC v. Rhode Island Board of Accountancy, 3 Trade Cas. (CCH) para.22,169 (Dkt. No. 9181—filed 1981) (February 12, 1985) (prohibition on advertising); (decision by administrative law judge holding no state action immunity); FTC v. Louisiana State Board of Dentistry, 3 Trade Cas. (CCH) para. 22,205 (Dkt. No. 9188-filed October 29, 1984) (restraint on dissemination of information on prices).

25. *See* Capital Telephone Co. v. N.Y. Telephone, 750 F.2d 373 (2d Cir. 1984); First American Title Co. of South Dakota v. South Dakota Land Title Association and South Dakota Abstractors Board of Examiners et al., 714 F.2d 1439 (8th Cir. 1983), *cert. denied*, 104 S.Ct. 709 (1984); Gambrel v. Kentucky Board of Dentistry, supra; *see also* Euster v. Eagle Downs Racing Association, 677 F.2d 813 (3rd Cir.), *cert. denied*, 450 U.S. 1022 (1982); Turf Paradise, Inc. v. Arizona Downs, 670 F.2d 813 (9th Cir. 1982); Horsemen's Benevolent and Protective Association v. Pennsylvania Horse Racing Commission, 530 F. Supp. 1098 (E.D. Pa. 1982) (horseracing; immune). *Compare* Morgan v. Division of Liquor Control, 664 F.2d 353 (3d Cir. 1981); Fisher Foods, Inc. v. Ohio Department of Liquor Control, 555 F. Supp. 641 (N.D. Ohio 1982); Hinshaw v. Beatrice Foods, Inc., 1980-81 Trade Cas. para. 63,584 (D. Mont. 1980) (comprehensive liquor regulation; immune) *with* Miller v. Oregon Liquor Control Commission, 688 F.2d 122 (9th Cir. 1982) (not comprehensive regulation; not immune).

26. *See* Mercy-Peninsula Ambulance v. County of San Mateo, 592 F. Supp. 956 (N.D. Cal. 1984).

27. See, *e.g.*, U.S. v. Title Insurance Rating Bureau of Arizona, 700 F.2d 1247 (9th Cir. 1983).

28. *See* Corey v. Look, 641 F.2d 32 (1st Cir. 1981).

29. Feminists Women's Health Center, Inc. v. Mohammad *supra*, Chapter I.

30. 105 S.Ct. 1713 (1985). In Garcia v. San Antonio Metropolitan Transit Authority, 105 S.Ct. 1005 (1985), the Supreme Court invalidated the test of "traditional governmental function" as a basis for commerce clause (including Sherman Act) immunity.

31. 105 S.Ct. at 1720 n.10.

32. *Id.*

33. 748 F.2d 373 (7th Cir. 1984).

34. 688 F.2d 122 (9th Cir. 1982).

35. 1984-2 Trade Cas. (CCH) para. 66,070 (App. Div. 2nd Dept., N.Y. 1984).

36. 740 F.2d 274 (4th Cir. 1984), *cert. denied*, 105 S.Ct. 561 (1985).

37. In addition to the state action doctrine, a second principle reflects considerations of state sovereignty. This principle, known as sovereign immunity, provides that an unconsenting state cannot be sued by a private citizen in a federal court. Moreover, state officials cannot be sued for monetary damages where the state is the real party in interest or the official is acting within their scope of authority. However, suits under federal law for future injunctive relief may be permitted in deference to federalism. Pennhurst State School & Hospital v. Halderman, 104 S.Ct. 900 (1984); Edelman v. Jordan, 415 U.S. 651 (1974); Ford Motor Co. v. Department of Treasury, 323 U.S. 459 (1965); Ex parte Young, 209 U.S. 123 (1908). Sovereign immunity, however, has been applied on occasion to bar antitrust actions, Mizlou Television v. National Broadcasting Co., 603 F. Supp. 677 (D.D.C. 1984), and has been distinguished to allow antitrust actions to proceed where officials are alleged to act outside the scope of their authority. *See* Bigelson v. Arizona Board of Medical Examiners, 1985-1 Trade Cas. (CCH) para. 66,488 (D. Ariz. 1985); Desoto Medical Center v. Methodist Hospital of Memphis, 604 F. Supp. 307 (S.D. Miss. 1985), or for injunctive relief, National Bank and Trust Co. v. Board of Regents, 1985-1 Trade Cas. (CCH) para. 66,462 (N.D. Ill. 1985). The application of sovereign immunity to antitrust law is uncertain at this juncture and boards should not rely unquestioningly on this defense.

38. 15 U.S.C. par. Section 1011-15.

39. 458 U.S. 119 (1982).

40. *Id.*

41. *See* Group Life & Health Insurance Co. v. Royal Drug Co., Inc., 440 U.S. 205 (1979); Virginia Academy of Clinical Psychologists v. Blue Shield of Virginia, 624 F.2d 476 (4th Cir. 1980), *cert. denied*, 450 U.S. 916 (1981); Ballard v. Blue Shield of S.W. Va., 543 F.2d 1075 (4th Cir. 1976), *cert. denied*, 430 U.S. 922 (1977); Nurse Midwifery Associates v. Hibbett, 549 F. Supp. 1185 (M.D. Tenn. 1982).

42. 458 U.S. at 129.

43. *See* Ratino v. Medical Service, 718 F.2d 1260 (4th Cir. 1983); Addino v. Genesse Valley Medical Care, Inc., 593 F. Supp. 892 (W.D.N.Y. 1984).

44. Harlow v. Fitzgerald, 457 U.S. 800 (1982); Wood v. Strickland, 420 U.S. 308, 320 (1975);

Scheuer v. Rhodes, 416 U.S. 232 (1974); *cf.* Hoke v. Board of Medical Examiners of State of North Carolina, 455 F. Supp. 1313 (D.N.C. 1978) (Civil Rights Act).

45. 586 F.2d 530 (5th Cir. 1978). *Cf.* Affiliated Capital Corp. v. City of Houston, 519 F. Supp. (S.D. Tex. 1981), *rev'd*, 700 F.2d 226 (5th Cir. 1983), *vacated* 714 F.2d 25 (5th Cir. 1983), *reversal aff'd en banc*, 735. 2d 1555 (5th Cir. 1984).

46. Health Care Equalization Comm. v. Iowa Medical Society, 501 F. Supp. 970 (S.D. Iowa 1980).

47. Allegheny Uniforms v. Howard Uniform Co., 384 F. Supp. 460 (W.D. Pa. 1974) (state port authority not entitled to dismiss action alleging conspiracy to limit purchase by state to one manufacturer).

48. Llewellyn v. Crothers, 1983-1 Trade Cas. (CCH) para. 65,358 (D. Ore. 1983).

49. Rogers v. Medical Association of Georgia, 259 S.E.2d 85 (1979) (statute which delegated decision of appointment of members of the Georgia State Board of Medical Examiners to the Medical Association of Georgia held unconstitutional).

CHAPTER THREE

Immunity For Petitioning the Government

One area of antitrust sensitivity is the relationship between individuals or associations and state boards. Associations are often groups of competitors who band together to seek advantage for their members, occasionally to the disadvantage of nonmembers. The antitrust laws contain an extensive interpretation of the limits on what associations of competitors (frequently with substantial market power and influence) can do. However, all groups and individuals have a right to petition the government for redress of grievances, a principle as old as the nation. Thus the antitrust laws are interpreted so as not to impair this basic First Amendment right to petition. The doctrine that private parties may generally go to the government to seek even anticompetitive relief against others without violating the antitrust laws is known as the *Noerr-Pennington* (referred to as the *Noerr*) doctrine.[1] This chapter explores the legitimate use of Noerr rights in approaches to boards and the areas in which petitioning conduct is not protected and can expose private parties and board members to antitrust liability.

Antitrust risk turns in large measure on the threefold rationale underlying *Noerr*. First, the purpose of the Sherman Act is to regulate business activity, not political activity. If private activity aimed at influencing government officials were to be subjected to antitrust scrutiny, the effect would be to overextend the reach of the commercial antitrust laws to *political* expression. Second, the imposition of antitrust liability could reduce the flow of needed information to the government and impair its ability to serve the public. Third, the activities of private parties in the process of petitioning the government are protected by the First Amendment.[2]

At the same time, *Noerr* rights are not unlimited. For example, intentional violations of due process, abuse of the governmental process, barring the access of competitors to the government, and private conspiratorial conduct all serve no legitimate governmental interest; if they are procured by private parties, *Noerr* may not provide any protection.

This chapter offers several illustrations of the considerable breadth of *Noerr* as well as examples of unprotected conduct of specific interest to board members.

In the *Noerr* case, several railroads advertised and lobbied to persuade the governor and legislature of Pennsylvania to restrict competition from the trucking industry in long distance heavy freight. The U.S. Supreme Court upheld the lobbying: "[w]e think it equally clear that the Sherman Act does not prohibit two or more persons from associating together in an attempt to persuade the legislature or the executive to take particular action with respect to a law that would produce a restraint or a monopoly."[3]

In the *Pennington* case, large mine owners and a union allegedly sought to impair the operations of small independent mines by convincing the secretary of labor to establish minimum wages which would be applicable to the small mines. The Supreme Court held these "joint efforts to influence public officials do not violate the antitrust laws even though intended to eliminate competition."[4] However, in *California Motor Transport Co. v. Trucking Unlimited*, one group of truckers allegedly conspired to undertake a campaign of baseless, repetitive state and federal proceedings to resist and defeat licensing applications necessary for the competitor to conduct business. The court ruled that "conspiracy with a licensing authority to eliminate a competitor may also result in an antitrust transgression."[5]

With this as background, other examples illustrate *Noerr* rights and the "sham" exception falling outside *Noerr's* protection.

Noerr Rights

In *First American Title Company of South Dakota v. South Dakota Land Title Association,*[6] the joint action by the South Dakota Abstractors Board of Examiners and individual South Dakota abstractors to amend a statute to favor and expand the business of South Dakota abstractors was held to be immune as *Noerr* petitioning conduct.

In *Federal Prescription Service v. American Pharmaceutical Association*,[7] the court found that *Noerr* protected both joint lobbying efforts by the National Association of State Boards of Pharmacy and the American Pharmaceutical Association directed at state boards of pharmacy seeking to inhibit mail order pharmaceutical sales and litigation in Iowa to enforce these rules.

Similarly, efforts by the Arkansas Dental Association in persuading the Arkansas Board of Dental Examiners to promulgate regulations restricting the practice of denturists were also held immune under *Noerr* in *Brazil v. Arkansas Board of Dental Examiners*.[8] Finally, in *Wheeling-Pittsburgh Steel Corporation v. Allied Trade and Conduit Corporation*,[9] *Noerr* protection was even extended to the lobbying of private standard-setting groups on which states rely.

The "Sham" Exception

The above situations illustrate the types of attempts to influence board rulemaking that are protected by the *Noerr* doctrine.

However, there are several limitations to the *Noerr* doctrine that are important to board members. A very important limitation is known as the "sham" exception. Under this principle, "a mere sham to cover what was actually nothing more than an attempt to interfere with the business relationship of a competition" is not protected under *Noerr*.[10]

In addition to conspiracy with a licensing authority to eliminate a competitor, the U.S. Supreme Court in *California Motor Transport* gave these examples of unprotected conduct: perjury of a witness; patent fraud; and bribery of a public purchasing agent.[11] Other unprotected conduct includes threats of violence by a union against state fair officials[12] and activity that bars access to the governmental process or abuses the due process rights of others. Such activity would include repetitive or baseless claims against a party in order to restrain their trade.[13] Several courts have also held that if private groups conspire with a governmental official, the conduct is not protected.[14]

One important issue of *Noerr* involvement arises when both private and governmental conduct are involved. Generally, *Noerr* would not protect private conspiratorial conduct which may have some governmental involvement.[15]

A second serious concern is the degree to which the *Noerr* doctrine protects state boards. Under current law, it is by no means clear that a state board's activity is entitled to any independent protection from antitrust liability under *Noerr-Pennington*. The doctrine serves to ensure the protection of private parties' constitutional rights and should not necessarily be extended to protect improper action by a state board. For example, in *Duke & Co., Inc. v. Forester*,[16] the court held that joint action among brewers, a public agency charged with the management of an airport, and a county commissioner to exclude competing brands of beer from the Pittsburgh airport was not within the state action doctrine and, thus, was not protected under *Noerr-Pennington*. The court stated:

Defendants contend that *Noerr-Pennington* immunity covers a state governmental entity which "listens to anti-competitive pleas."

Doubtlessly, this proposition is correct so long as the public body acts within its legal discretion and in what it considers the public interest.

Where the complaint goes beyond mere allegations of official persuasion by anti-competitive lobbying and claims official participation with private individuals in a scheme to restrain trade, the *Noerr-Pennington* doctrine is inapplicable.[17]

Conclusion

The *Noerr* doctrine reaffirms that our system is based upon the right of citizens to have a voice in their government and to petition it to obtain certain governmental conduct. But *Noerr* does not authorize otherwise illegal conduct. Indeed, some courts have found that the *Noerr-Pennington* doctrine is limited to the "need of the governmental units for citizen input in making decisions that [the state action doctrine] holds to be outside the scope of the Sherman Act."[18] If that conclusion is correct, it may be that the scope of *Noerr-Pennington* would be no broader than the state action doctrine protections extended to state boards. At least until there is more consistent authority than currently exists, state occupational licensing boards should not assume that *Noerr-Pennington* will provide them with insulation from antitrust liability in situations where their conduct falls outside the state action doctrine. There is very clearly no basis for a state occupational licensing board to believe that it will be exempt from antitrust liability merely because it has acted in response to requests of private parties. Moreover, where the board's conduct seems to regulate the "commercial" aspects of a profession, regardless at whose behest, *Noerr* may be irrelevant.

The application of *Noerr* to state boards remains open. In the meantime, adherence to stated rules to provide equal access to all interested parties and to meet expectations about even-handed decision making can provide protection and promote sound decision making.

Notes

1. Eastern Railroad President Conference v. Noerr Motor Freight, Inc., 365 U.S. 27, 135 (1961); United Mine Workers v. Pennington, 381 U.S. 657 (1965).

2. Some courts have therefore said that *Noerr* protects "political" but not "commercial" activity. *Compare* State of Missouri v. National Organization of Women, Inc., 620 F.2d 1301 (D.C. Cir. 1980), *cert. denied*, 449 U.S. 842 (1981) ("political" activity protected) with Whitten v. Paddock Pool Builders, 424 F. 2d 25, 31-33 (1st Cir.), *cert. denied*, 400 U.S. 850 ("commercial" activity not protected).

3. 365 U.S. at 136.

4. 381 U.S. at 670.

5. 404 U.S. 508, 513 (1972).

6. 714 F.2d 1439 (8th Cir. 1983).

7. 471 F. Supp. 126 (D.D.C. 1970), *rev'd*, 663 F.2d 262 (D.C. Cir. 1981), *cert. denied*, 455 U.S. 928 (1982). A legal theory for challenging state boards for conduct allegedly falling outside of *Noerr* is set forth in detail in the trial court opinion, which was reversed partly on the facts on appeal. The appellate court held that *Noerr* conduct was immune and the alleged non-*Noerr* conspiratorial conduct was not proven.

8. Brazil v. Arkansas Board of Dental Examiners, 593 F. Supp. 1354 (E.D. Ark. 1984); *see also* Bank Building and Equipment Corporation of America v. National Council of Architectural Registration Boards, 1975-1 Trade Cas. (CCH) para. 60,108 (D.D.C. 1978).

9. 573 F. Supp. 833 (N.D. Ill. 1983).

10. 365 U.S. at 144.

11. 404 U.S. at 512-13.

12. Sacramento Coca-Cola Bottling Co. v. Chauffeurs, etc., 440 F.2d 1096 (9th Cir. 1971).

13. *See* California Motor transport, *supra*; Otter Tail Power Co. v. United States, 410 U.S. 366 (1973); Clipper Exxpress v. Rocky Mountain Motor Tariff Bureau, 690 F. 2d 1240 (9th Cir. 1982), *cert. denied*, 103 S. Ct. 1234 (1983); Feminist Women's Health Center, Inc. v. Mohammad, 586 F.2d 530, 542-43 n.6 (5th Cir. 1978), *cert. denied*, 444 U.S. 924 (1979).

14. See also California Motor Transport, *supra*; In re Airport Car Rental, 521 F. Supp. 568, 588 (N.D. Cal. 1981), *aff'd*, 693 F.2d 84 (9th Cir. 1982); Federal Prescription Service, Inc. v. American Pharmaceutical Ass'n, 484 F. Supp. 1195, 1202-04, 1209 (D.D.C. 1980), *aff'd in part, rev'd in part*, 663 F. 253, 267 (D.C. Cir.), *cert. denied*, 455 U.S. 928 (1982); Kurek v. Pleasure Driveway & Park District, 557 F.2d 580, 593-94 (7th Cir. 1977), *vacated and remanded*, 435 U.S. 992 (1978), *reinstated*, 583 F.2d 378 (7th Cir. 1978), *cert. denied*, 439 U.S. 1090 (1979); Duke & Co. v. Foerster, 521 F.2d 1277, 1282 (3rd Cir. 1975).

15. *E.g.* Virginia Academy of Clinical Psychologists v. Blue Shield, 624 F.2d 476 (4th Cir. 1980), *cert. denied*, 450 U.S. 916 (1981).

16. 521 F.2d 1277 (3rd Cir. 1975). However, other cases take a different view from *Duke* and reject the co-conspirator exception. *See, e.g.*, First American Title Company of S. Dakota v. S. Dakota Title Ass'n., 714 F.2d 1439 (8th Cir. 1983); Westborough Mall, Inc. v. City of Cape Giradeau, 683 F.2d 733 (8th Cir. 1982), *cert. denied*, 461 U.S. 945 (1983); Metrocable Co. v. CATV of Rockford, 516 F.2d 220 (7th Cir. 1975).

17. 521 F.2d at 1282.

18. Kurek v. Pleasure Driveway and Park District of Peoria, *supra*, 557 F.2d at 593.

CHAPTER FOUR

Due Process, Equal Protection and Rational Basis

In the first chapter, we discussed the competition policy questions raised by antitrust law and the First Amendment. The issue of *whether* anticompetitive regulatory decisions should occur—and if so, in what form and degree—often depends upon the *manner* in which decisions are made by regulators. We continue this discussion with several related areas of competitive concern: due process (fair procedures); equal protection (fair treatment of people or groups which are of substantially equivalent qualifications); and the doctrine that there must be a rational basis to sustain rulemaking.

The first two doctrines are principles of constitutional law. They have not frequently been interpreted in the context of antitrust litigation against state boards, and there are substantial questions as to their general applicability in this setting. However, they have been applied (particularly due process) in the area of private standard setting. This chapter does *not* suggest that a due process denial in state regulation, by itself, creates antitrust exposure. However, because of the role of due process and equal protection in the formulation of state competition policy, these principles are considered here. The chapter begins with a brief introductory discussion of some private litigation raising the competitive issues followed by several specific illustrations.

In *American Society of Mechanical Engineers v. Hydrolevel Corporation*,[1] states relied upon a private standard-setting association of competitors which established standards for hot water boiler safety devices. Using a combination of conflicts of interest, denial of due process and secrecy, volunteer agents of the private group intentionally formulated an erroneous interpretation of a private standard which prevented an innovator from competing and drove it out of business. The innovator brought an antitrust suit against the association and recovered a judgment for treble damages against it. In *Hydrolevel*, the reliance of state and local codes and boards on compliance with the standards as a condition of sale provided part of the market power which enabled the scheme to succeed.

In *Silver v. New York Stock Exchange*,[2] competing members of the New York Stock Exchange terminated essential wire services to nonmembers without any due process hearing, which impaired the business of some and terminated the business of other nonmembers. The nonmembers brought an antitrust suit and the U.S. Supreme Court ruled the conduct to be an unlawful group boycott, noting that the Exchange had a duty to regulate with due process since the exchange had such a dominant position. Also in *Gibson v. Berryhill*,[3] the Supreme Court held it to be a violation of due process where individual optometrists in Alabama completely controlled a state board which established rules and determined the suitability of competing "corporate" optometrists to be licensed and disciplined. Although a due process case, *Gibson v. Berryhill* has implications for state competition policy and was relied on by the Supreme Court in the *Goldfarb* case.

Taken together, these cases illustrate the general observation that due process helps assure that competitive decisions are made openly and that the basis of decision is clear. However, this general observation is subject to several immediate qualifications in the area of state regulation. Court decisions involving due process denials have not been applied to impose antitrust damage liability on states or state officials. These decisions involve private action by commercial competitors; in occupational licensure the government interest is not furthered by procedural errors or impediments to competition. Even if due process is denied, a state board arguably acts unilaterally or in any event makes no agreement with a necessary second party to violate the antitrust laws. However, in *U.S. v. Mississippi State Board of Professional Engineers and Land Surveyors*, the Justice Department has argued that a state licensing board composed of practitioners in and of itself satisfies the agreement requirement. (*See also Nurse Midwifery Associates v. Hibbitt*). Some decisions after *Gibson v. Berryhill* have allowed considerable latitude in the selection of board members with ties to professional associations where the association is not given power of selection. Finally, the whole inquiry may be moot where the board's activities are immune as state action or the association's conduct is immune as petitioning the government. Board conduct is very clearly protected in the area of due process disciplinary proceedings for incompetent practice. In antitrust terms, discipline of incompetent practitioners in these circumstances is arguably not a "restraint" at all or is reasonable because discipline addresses only allegations of unlawful conduct, and it may be immune as state action. Furthermore, this issue of inadvertent due process denial is different from intentional use of a disciplinary mechanism with the purpose or effect of improperly restraining the trade of other practitioners.

Future case law will probably contain additional interpretation regarding any antitrust implications of due process denial by state boards. However, because the issue has arisen with regard to private standard setting, many boards are concerned that due process be afforded in rulemaking, licensure, and discipline. Although the requirements of each state may differ with regard to specific procedural issues, and this section is not comprehensive, we will discuss several common areas of due process rulemaking concern.

Several Illustrations

Let us suppose that your board is considering writing a regulation in which the scope of practice is at issue. A "dominant" profession introduces rulemaking evidence to show that profession's capability, historical presence in the field, and safety. This evidence is used to support a claim to licensure with a substantial and exclusive scope of practice.

At this juncture, two observations are important. First, the record thus far should not determine any possible definitions which the board is evaluating. This record contains no information regarding the capability, training, safety and other factors important to the board, the public and the allied profession regarding other competitive alternatives. Unless the public, the allied profession and other interested parties have due process notice of the rulemaking and an opportunity to be heard objectively, the rulemaking may omit this evidence and may result in highly anticompetitive regulation serving the economic interests of the dominant profession but not other interests. Denial of the right to be apprised of and be heard on the proposal would deny due process.

Due process includes *notice* and the *opportunity to be heard*. While these factors depend in part on the circumstances of particular administrative situations, the following hypothetical examples will further illustrate due process and the observation that rulemaking due process requirements are often more general than those applicable to discipline. We will discuss five factors that promote due process rulemaking: (1) the notice; (2) a hearing; (3) a neutral decision-maker; (4) freedom from *ex parte* communications and (5) review. These, in turn, promote informed competition policy.

Notice

Example: The State Board of Pharmacy is considering promulgating a regulation on short notice. The regulation would prohibit use of trade names and provide that in the case of a disciplinary proceeding against a pharmacist, the pharmacist would be given notice of a hearing by published notice in the local newspaper on the date before the hearing. The notice would include the name of the pharmacist and the location, date and time of the hearing. In order to avoid potential embarrassment to the pharmacist, the notice would not include any statement of the nature of the charges against the pharmacist or the legal or factual basis for the proposed disciplinary action.

Implicit in the concept of "opportunity to be heard" is the requirement that a person be given notice in a manner reasonably calculated to inform the person of the pending action and sufficient to enable the person to participate in the rulemaking or to prepare a defense to disciplinary charges. The issues relevant to the notice requirement are the manner of giving notice, the timing of the notice, and the contents of the notice. The example described above is fatally deficient for several reasons.

In rulemaking, notice by publication should be supplemented by individual written notice to affected groups, including consumer groups. As a general rule, notice by publication alone is considered inadequate in disciplinary proceedings because as a practical matter it is not reasonable to assume that the individual will read the published notice.[4] Personal notice is more likely to ensure that the individual is in fact notified and is therefore generally required in matters of discipline.

With respect to the questions of the timing of the notice, one day is clearly insufficient. Problems can be avoided by assuring ample time is available and by liberally granting extensions of time when requested for the purpose of obtaining counsel or otherwise preparing for the hearing.

A rulemaking notice should describe (with particularity if possible) the object of and background information about the proceeding. In discipline matters, it is well settled that the notice must include a statement of charges that is sufficiently detailed to permit the individual to prepare a defense.[5] Both the factual and legal basis of the charges should be stated in the notice. It is not necessary to outline the evidence which will be presented at the hearing, but a summary of the basis of the charges must be included.

Hearing

Example: In an effort to streamline the disciplinary process for violations of its standards, a state licensing board proposes a rule to set forth the following procedure to be followed at disciplinary hearings. The attorney for the state will summarize the evidence which supports the imposition of disciplinary action. The individual will then have an opportunity to state the reasons that discipline should not be imposed. Neither side shall present the testimony of witnesses and neither side shall interrogate the other's representative.

Rulemaking on disciplinary procedures can be a source of confusion because different principles may be applicable to rulemaking and discipline. For this reason, we have selected and will work through this example.

While a state licensing board proceeding need not be conducted with all the formal trappings of a full-blown judicial proceeding, certain procedural safeguards are fundamental to a fair hearing even if many of the formalities are not required.

First, parties in rulemaking should be permitted to be represented by counsel. In disciplinary proceedings themselves,it is clear that the individual has the right to be represented by counsel at all stages of the proceeding.[6] This right does not carry with it a concomitant right to have counsel appointed on the individual's behalf, but is merely the right to retain counsel. Once counsel is present, the licensing board should communicate through counsel, rather than directly with the individual.

Second, although cross-examination in rulemaking may not be essential, each group should have the right to respond to or comment on the record. In disciplinary proceedings, the right to confront adverse witnesses is a fundamental due process right and may not be eliminated.[7] The individual must have the opportunity to cross-examine those persons who testify against him or her. In addition, there must be an opportunity to present witnesses on his or her own behalf.[8]

There may be variations in the manner of the presentation of evidence depending on the significance of the issues involved in a given hearing. Some administrative proceedings may be amenable to a procedure that calls for the presentation of one's position in writing. However, for a proceeding that involves issues as significant as individuals' rights to practice their occupation, an actual hearing is probably mandated by the due process clause and is at the least very strongly recommended.

Neutral and Detached Decision Maker

Example: The State Board of Optometry is composed solely of private solo practitioners. The board is adopting and implementing a corporate employment and advertising rule. Under the rule, the board will initiate disciplinary proceedings to revoke the licenses of optometrists who violated the provision, which includes almost one-half of the optometrists practicing in the state. Following a hearing on each individual case, the board will decide on the issue of revoking the particular optometrist's license.[9]

Although not necessarily a strict requirement of due process, rulemaking is more likely to be objective if the board consists of either disinterested parties or is balanced by members not directly affected by the rulemaking. A fundamental element of a constitutionally valid disciplinary hearing is a neutral and detached decision maker. Where the decision maker has a pecuniary interest in the matter to be decided, the principles of due process require that the adjudicator be disqualified.[10] In a factual situation similar to that described above, the U.S. Supreme Court found that the members of the board, all of whom were optometrists in private practice, could financially benefit from a ruling which would lead to the revocation of the licenses of a large number of competing optometrists in the state. Even such an indirect pecuniary interest on the part of the board was sufficient to raise substantial questions about the neutrality of the board and therefore the use of such a board as adjudicator was constitutionally impermissible. Careful attention by the governor's office should be given to the selection process, composition and qualification of board members to help assure informed and objective rulemaking and other decision making.

The issue of the objectivity of the decision maker often arises in regulatory systems where the same person who prosecutes and/or investigates the particular case acts as judge in the matter. While the Supreme Court has not ruled on these issues,[11] it is clear that due process questions arise whenever a licensing board investigates a matter, initiates a prosecution on the basis of the investigation and then sits as an adjudicative body to decide the material facts in the case. The potential problem is one of bias and prejudgment. In order to ensure that an individual's due process rights are not violated, the preferred position is for a licensing board to appoint a neutral hearing examiner who is not otherwise associated with the board. Some states have begun the use of hearing examiners in this type of situation to avoid any question that arises from the merging of investigatory and/or prosecutorial functions with adjudicative functions.

Ex parte Communications

Example: Following the hearing on the issue of the revocation of a physician's license to practice medicine, the hearing examiner appointed by the Board of Medical Examiners decides that he needs more information in order to decide the case. Without notifying the physician, he contacts other physicians in the community who provide him with the necessary additional information to make an informed decision.

A basic rule central to our system of justice is that the judge or other decision maker shall not communicate with anyone concerning any aspect of a matter which is before him unless both sides of the dispute are present. Communications between the judge and one side of a dispute or even third-party communications are strictly forbidden in all judicial proceedings. The reason for this strict rule is that the opportunity for bias is minimized if both parties are present whenever any evidence or argument is being presented to the judge. This is an important element in our adversarial system and is necessary to maintain its integrity.

In administrative proceedings as well as in judicial proceedings, the rule against *ex parte* communications is strictly enforced.[12] If there is any violation of the due process rights of the individual in the procedures, any decision which follows such a proceeding will be overruled even though there may be sufficient other evidence to sustain or uphold the decision. Although the courts have not ruled extensively on the issue, *ex parte* (or other) unauthorized or intentional misconduct to the competitive disadvantage of others may raise antitrust issues.

Judicial Review

Example: State regulation provides that a certified public accountant whose license to practice accounting is revoked shall have the right to appeal that decision to the intermediate appellate court in the state.

The U.S. Supreme Court has not ruled that the constitutional guarantee of due process of law requires judicial review of an administrative decision. However, the right to appellate review in the courts as to rulemaking and discipline is strongly recommended, although it may not be essential to ensure due process.[13]

Equal Protection and Rational Basis

In addition to procedural due process as a requirement for fair occupational licensure, treating persons of equal skill in a similar manner is also a standard of fairness. To do otherwise is inequitable to licensees and deprives the public of cost-effective competitive choices among competent personnel. Scope of practice standards are a frequent source of these issues. Legislatures and boards can draw rational distinctions between different categories of personnel. Equal protection and rational basis issues raise the question: Is this distinction legitimate and can it be sustained? The question is important since distinctions which deny equal protection or lack of rational basis may be struck down.

Legislatures have great leeway in making choices. In *New Orleans* v. *Dukes*,[14] the U.S. Supreme Court explained the purpose of equal protection as follows:

> When local economic regulation is challenged solely as violating the Equal Protection Clause, this Court consistently defers to legislative determinations as to the desirability of particular statutory discriminations . . . . Unless a classification trammels fundamental personal rights or is drawn upon inherently suspect distinctions such as race, religion, or alienage, our decisions presume the constitutionality of the statutory discriminations and require only that the classification challenged be rationally related to a legitimate state interest.[15]

The right to specific occupational licensure is not "fundamental" in the constitutional sense as are free speech and political rights. The standard for review for regulatory purposes is whether there is a rational basis for the classification in question.[16] The rational basis test requires that state regulatory action be rationally related to the accomplishment of a legitimate state purpose based on promotion of the public welfare, health or safety.[17] Moreover, state classifications are assumed to be valid and are not overturned on equal protection grounds "unless the varying treatment of different groups or persons is so unrelated to the achievement of any combination of legitimate purposes that we can only conclude that the legislature's actions were irrational."[18]

In reviewing the rationality of a classification, a court may even hypothesize legislative purposes: "Where there are plausible reasons for Congress' action, our inquiry is at an end. It is, of course, constitutionally irrelevant whether this reasoning in fact underlay the legislative decision . . . because this court has never insisted that a legislative body articulate its reasons for enacting a statute."[19]

Conclusion

In general, the courts have been especially deferential to legislative classifications in cases of challenges to the state regulation of licensed professions.[20] In sum, unless the classification bears no relation to skill or trade involved (such as citizenship or sex), a classification will probably be upheld unless it has no defensible reason that can be articulated. In rulemaking, however, the courts are less deferential and apply a rational basis test.[21] (No view is expressed in the *Manual* as to the implications for antitrust immunity or other exposure for conduct taken under state legislation or regulation which is invalidated as either violating equal protection or lacking a rational basis.)

Regardless of the antitrust implications, however, state competition policy is promoted by assurance of due process, equal protection and rational rulemaking. An open process encouraging full participation during the formulation of legislation and rulemaking can help assure that these principles are recognized. This approach provides a scientific, systematic process which encourages professions to compete on the basis of competence and to have this competence recognized in state regulation.

Notes

1. 456 U.S. 556 (1982).

2. 341 U.S. 773 (1962). In Pacific Stationery & Printing Co. v. Northwest Wholesale Stationers, 53 U.S.L.W. 4733 (1985), the Court limited *Silver* to cases where expulsion was likely to have an anticompetitive effect. In other situations a plaintiff seeking application of the *per se* rule must make a threshold showing that the challenged conduct is the type that is likely to have predominantly anticompetitive effect.

3. 411 U.S. 564 (1973).

4. Mullane v. Central Hanover Bank & Trust Co., 339 U.S. 306 (1950).

5. Goldberg v. Kelly, 397 U.S. 254, 268 (1970); Armstrong v. Manso, 380 U.S. 552 (1965).

6. Mosley v. St. Louis Southwestern-Railway, 634 F.2d 942 (5th Cir. 1981).

7. Goldberg v. Kelly, 397 U.S. at 268-269.

8. *Id.*

9. This was the factual situation in Gibson v. Berryhill, 411 U.S. 564 (1973).

10. *Id.*; *see also* Ward v. Village of Monroeville, 409 U.S. 57 (1972); Tumey v. Ohio, 273 U.S. 510 (1927).

11. The Supreme Court has expressly refrained from deciding that the merging of prosecutorial, investigative and adjudicative functions is necessarily a violation of due process. 411 U.S. at 579, n.17 (1973).

12. *See generally* 3 K. Davis, Administrative Law Treatise Par. 18.7 (2d ed. 1980); Home Box Office, Inc. v. F.C.C., 567 F.2d 9 (D.C. Cir. 1977).

13. *Cf.* Ortwein v. Schwab, 410 U.S. 656, 660 (1973).

14. 427 U.S. 297 (1976).

15. *Id.* at 303.

16. Vance v. Bradley, 440 U.S. 93, 97 (1979).

17. *See e.g.* Rinaldi v. Yaeger, 384 U.S. 305, 309-10 (1966).

18. Barry v. Barchi, 443 U.S. 55, 67 (1979).

19. United States Railroad Retirement Board v. Fritz, 449 U.S. 166, 179 (1980).

20. *See e.g.*, Watson v. Maryland, 218 U.S. 173 (1910); Williamson v. Lee Optical Co. 348 U.S. 483 (1955); Ohralik v. State Bar Assn., 436 U.S. 447, 460 (1978).

21. Some authorities evaluating this general problem include: Szeto v. Louisiana Board of Dentistry, 508 F. Supp. 268 (E.D. La. 1981); Wong v. Hohnstrom, 405 F. Supp. 727 (D. Minn. 1975); Surmeli v. State of New York, 412 F. Supp. 394 (S.D.N.Y. 1976); Tozzoli v. Killiam, 386 F. Supp. 9 (D. Conn. 1974). *Compare* Oliver v. Norton, 361 F. Supp. 1362 (D. Ga. 1973) *with* Brandwein v. Cal. Bd. of Osteopathic Examiners, 708 F. 2d 1466 (9th Cir. 1983); Maceluch v. Wyson, 680 F.2d 1062 (5th Cir. 1982); Procario v. Ambach, 561 F. Supp. 804 (N.D.N.Y. 1983); *see also* Eatough v. Albano, 673 F. 2d 671 (3rd Cir. 1982), *cert. denied*, 457 U.S. 1119 (1983) (M.D. versus D.O. degrees): Forman v. Ambach, 525 F. Supp 722 (N.D.N.Y. 1976) (different disciplinary procedures for physicians and attorneys); Gold Cross Ambulance v. City of Kansas City, 538 F.Supp. 956 (W.D. Mo. 1982), *aff'd* 705 F.2d 1005 (8th Cir. 1983), *cert. denied*, 105 S. Ct. 1864 (1985) (dual standards for licensing); Wall & Ochs, Inc. v. Hicks, 469 F. Supp. 873 (D.N.C. 1970 (exemption for certain groups in dispensing eyeglasses); *cf.* Wall & Ochs, Inc. v. Grosso, 469 F. Supp. 1088 (D. Conn. 1979) (claim that 4-year apprenticeship and examination requirement had no rational connection with applicant's capacity to practice as an optician).

CHAPTER FIVE
Conclusion

During the course of this *Manual*, several concerns have been addressed. The power of the state to promote (or thwart) competition among competent professionals is a pervasive theme. For this reason, we began by briefly describing the concerns of the antitrust and several other relevant laws in this area, with specific illustrations of how competitive issues can arise in state regulation. To encourage analysis of these choices, we have provided a sample list of questions in Chapter One which reflect these concerns. At the same time, the federal system grants further powers to the states in the form of immunity under both the state action doctrine and for petitioning the government. As we have indicated, however, these doctrines are not without limits. The course of state regulation requires fairness to all participants, and the discussion of the importance of due process, equal protection, and rational basis considerations throughout the process have been explored.

The *Manual* is a point of departure. New decisions and even new doctrines will influence the course of state professional regulation. The *Manual* is a beginning and not the end of analysis. It is a pause to take stock and foster discussion, a point of departure as state professional regulation enters the second decade after the *Goldfarb* case. A review of the text and authorities in the *Manual* will reflect the intensity of activity in this initial period. The level of activity and the new requirements of law underscore the importance that boards periodically give serious reconsideration to their enabling legislation and regulations to protect not only the public but their own processes, members and staff.

Public protection requires objective evaluation at the rulemaking stage. However, a system of evaluation of competence requires a strong disciplinary program where there is reason to question the competence of a practitioner. Proper discipline is procompetitive and is lawful under the antitrust laws. The development and maintenance of a rigorous discipline program is a matter of priority for every state concerned with the quality of its own competition policy and protection of its residents and visitors.[1]

Professional regulation is a major public responsibility. We hope this *Manual* will assist you in implementing the basic democractic and professional values of your state and profession.

Note

1. *See Disciplinary Action Manual for Occupational Licensing Boards* (National Association of Attorneys General Committee on the Office of Attorney General 1978); *Occupational Licensing Enforcement: Guidelines to the Investigator* (The Council of State Governments 1982).

Two recent monographs which may be of particular interest to members of state medical and other health professional boards are R. J. Feinstein, *Special Report: The Ethics of Professional Regulation*, 312 N. Engl. J. Med. 801-04 (1985) and A. S. Relman, *Professional Regulation and the State Medical Boards*, 312 N. Engl. J. Med. 784-85 (1985).

Appendix I

Selected State Antitrust Statutes and Constitutional Provisions

Alabama
Ala. Code sec. 8-10-1 (1975)

Alaska
Alaska Stat. sec. 45.50.562 et seq. (1984)

Arizona
Ariz. Rev. Stat. Ann. sec. 44-1401 et seq. (1968)

Arkansas
Ark. Stat. Ann. sec. 70-101 et seq. (1979)

California
Cal. Bus. and Prof. Code sec. 16720 (West 1964)

Colorado
Colo. Rev. Stat. 6-4-101 et seq. (1973)

Connecticut
Conn. Gen. Stat. Ann. 35-24 et seq. (1984 Supp.)

District of Columbia
D.C. Code Ann. sec. 28-4501 et seq. (1981)

Florida
Fla. Stat. Ann. sec. 542.15 et seq. (West 1980)

Georgia
Ga. Constit. art. III sec. VI, para. V(c) (1983); Ga. Code 13-8-2 (1982)

Hawaii
Hawaii Rev. Stat. sec. 480-4 et seq. (1976)

Idaho
Idaho Code sec. 48-101 et seq. (1977)

Illinois
Ill. S.H.A. Chap. 60 sec. 1 et seq.

Indiana
Ind. Code sec. 24-1 et seq. (1964)

Iowa
Iowa Code Ann. sec. 553.1 et seq. (West 1977)

Kansas
Kan. Stat. Ann. sec. 50-112 (1983)

Kentucky
Ky. Rev. Stat. Ann. sec. 367.175 (1976)

Louisiana
La. Rev. Stat. Ann. RS 51-122 et seq. (West 1968)

Maine
Me. Rev. Stat. Ann. tit. 10 sec. 1101 (1980)

Maryland
Md. Com. Law Code Ann. sec. 11-201 et seq. (1983)

Massachusetts
Mass. Gen. Laws Ann. Ch. 93 sec. 1 et seq. (West 1978)

Michigan
Mich. Stat. Ann. sec. 445.701 et seq. (Callahan 1967)

Minnesota
Minn. Stat. Ann. sec. 325D.49 (West 1981)

Mississippi
Miss. Code Ann. sec. 75-21-1 (1972)

Missouri
Mo. Rev. Stat. sec. 416.031 et seq. (1977)

Montana
Mont. Code. Ann. sec. 30-14-205 (1981)

Nebraska
Neb. Rev. Stat sec. 59-801 et seq. (1968)

Nevada
Nev. Rev. Stat. sec. 598.410 (1979) (deceptive trade practices)

New Hampshire
N.H. Rev. Stat. Ann. sec. 356.1 et seq. (1966)

New Jersey
N.J. Stat. Ann. 56:9-1 et seq. (West 1984 supp.)

New Mexico
N.M. Stat. Ann. sec. 57-1-1 et seq. (1978)

New York
N.Y. Gen. Bus. Law sec. 340 et seq. (McKinney 1968)

North Carolina
N.C. Gen. Stat. sec. 75-1 et seq. (1965)

North Dakota
N.D. Cent. Code sec. 51-08-01 et seq.

Ohio
Ohio Rev. Code Ann. sec. 1331.01 et seq. (Baldwin 1962)

Oklahoma
Okla. Stat. Ann. tit. 79 sec. et seq. (West 1971 supp.)

Oregon
Or. Rev. Stat. sec. 646.705 et seq. (1979)

Pennsylvania
Pa. Stat. Ann. tit. 73 sec. 213 (Purdon 1971)

Rhode Island
R.I. Gen Laws sec. 6.13-1.2 (1969) (deceptive trade practices)

South Carolina
S.C. Code Ann. sec. 39-3-10 (Law. Co-op 1977)

South Dakota
S.D. Comp. Laws Ann. sec. 37-1-3.1 (1977)

Tennessee
Tenn. Code Ann. sec. 47-25-101 et seq.

Texas
Tex. Bus. & Commerce Code Ann. sec. 15.01 et seq. (Vernon 1968)

Utah
Utah Code Ann. sec. 76-10-911 et seq. (1983 Supp.)

Vermont
Vt. Stat. Ann. tit. 29 sec. 908 (1970)

Virginia
Va. Code sec. 59.1-9.1 et seq. (1968)

Washington
Wash. Constit. art. XII sec. 22 (1973)

West Virginia
W.Va. Code sec. 47-18-1 et seq. (1978)

Wisconsin
Wis. Stat. Ann. sec. 133.01 et seq. (West 1974)

Wyoming
Wyo. Const. art. 1 sec. 30 and art. 10 sec. 8

Appendix II
Selected Federal Antitrust Laws

Sherman Act

Section I

Every contract, combination in the form of trust or otherwise, or conspiracy, in restraint of trade or commerce among the several States, or with foreign nations, is hereby declared to be illegal. Every person who shall make any contract or engage in any combination or conspiracy hereby declared to be illegal shall be deemed guilty of a felony, and, on conviction thereof, shall be punished by fine not exceeding one million dollars if a corporation, or, if any other person, one hundred thousand dollars, or by imprisonment not exceeding three years, or by both said punishments, in the discretion of the court. [15 U.S.C. sec. 1]

Section 2

Every person who shall monopolize, or attempt to monopolize, or combine or conspire with any other person or persons, to monopolize any part of the trade or commerce among the several States, or with foreign nations, shall be deemed guilty of a felony, and, on conviction thereof, shall be punished by fine not exceeding one million dollars if a corporation, or, if any other person, one hundred thousand dollars, or by imprisonment not exceeding three years, or by both said punishments, in the discretion of the court. [15 U.S.C. sec. 2]

Section 8

That the word "person," or "persons," wherever used in this act shall be deemed to include corporations and associations existing under or authorized by the laws of either the United States, the laws of any of the Territories, the laws of any State, or the laws of any foreign country. [15 U.S.C. sec. 7]

Clayton Act

Section 4

(a) Except as provided in subsection (b), any person who shall be injured in his business or property by reason of anything forbidden in the antitrust laws may sue therefor in any district court of the United States in the district in which the defendant resides or is found or has an agent, without respect to the amount in controversy, and shall recover threefold the damages by him sustained, and the cost of suit, including a reasonable attorney's fee. [15 U.S.C. sec. 15]

Section 4A

Whenever the United States is hereafter injured in its business or property by reason of anything forbidden in the antitrust laws it may sue therefor in the United States district court for the district in which the defendant resides or is found or has an agent, without respect to the amount in controversy, and shall recover actual damages by it sustained and the cost of suit. [15 U.S.C. sec. 15a]

Section 4C

(a)(1) Any Attorney General of a State may bring a civil action in the name of such State, as parens patriae on behalf of natural persons residing in such State, in any district court of the United States having jurisdiction of the defendant, to secure monetary relief as provided in this section for injury sustained by such natural persons to their property by reason of any violation of the Sherman Act. [15 U.S.C. sec. 15c]

Section 4F

(a) Whenever the Attorney General of the United States has brought an action under the antitrust laws, and he has reason to believe that any State attorney general would be entitled to bring an action under this Act based substantially on the same alleged violation of the antitrust laws, he shall promptly give written notification thereof to such State attorney general.

(b) To assist a State attorney general in evaluating the notice or in bringing any action under this Act, the Attorney General of the United States shall, upon request by such State attorney general, make available to him, to the extent permitted by law, any investigative files or other materials which are or may be relevant or material to the actual or potential cause of action under this Act. [15 U.S.C. sec. 15f]

Clayton Act (as amended)

Local Government Antitrust Act of 1984

Public Law 98-544
98th Congress

An Act

To clarify the application of the Clayton Act to the official conduct of local governments, and for other purposes.

Be it enacted by the Senate and House of Representatives of the United States of America in Congress assembled. That this act may be cited as the "Local Government Antitrust Act of 1984."

Sec. 2. For purposes of this Act—(1) the term "local government" means—

(A) a city, county, parish, town, township, village, or any other general function governmental unit established by State law, or

(B) a school district, sanitary district, or any other special function governmental unit established by State law in one or more States.

(2) the term "person" has the meaning given it in subsection (a) of the first section of the Clayton Act (15 U.S.C. 12(A)), but does not include any local government as defined in paragraph (1) of this section, and

(3) the term "State" has the meaning given it in section 4G(2) of the Clayton Act (15 U.S.C. 15g(2)).

Sec. 3. (a) No damages, interest on damages, costs, or attorney's fees may be recovered under section 4, 4A, or 4C of the Clayton Act (15 U.S.C. 15, 15a, or 15c) from any local government, or official or employee thereof acting in an official capacity.

(b) Subsection (a) shall not apply to cases commenced before the effective date of this Act unless the defendant establishes and the court determines, in light of all the circumstances, including the stage of litigation and the availability of alternative relief under the Clayton Act, that it would be inequitable not to apply this subsection to a pending case. In consideration of this section, existence of a jury verdict, district court judgment, or any stage of litigation subsequent thereto, shall be deemed to be prima facie evidence that subsection (a) shall not apply.

Sec. 4. (a) No damages, interest on damages, costs or attorney's fees may be recovered under section 4, 4A or 4C of the Clayton Act (15 U.S.C. 15,

15a, or 15c) in any claim against a person based on any official action directed by a local government, or official or employee thereof acting in an official capacity.

(b) Subsection (a) shall not apply with respect to cases commenced before the effective date of this Act.

Sec. 5. Section 510 of the Departments of Commerce, Justice, and State, the Judiciary, and Related Agencies Appropriation Act, 1985 (Public Law 98-411) is repealed. Sec. 6. This Act shall take effect thirty days before the date of the enactment of this Act.

Approved October 24, 1984.

Federal Trade Commission Act

(Excerpts)

Section 4 Definition

The words defined in this section shall have the following meaning when found in this Act [15 USCS Sections 41 et seq.], to wit:
"Corporation" shall be deemed to include any company, trust, so-called Massachusetts trust, or association, incorporated or unincorporated, which is organized to carry on business for its own profit or that of its members, and has shares of capital or capital stock or certificates of interest, and any company, trust, so-called Massachusetts trust, or association, incorporated or unincorporated, without shares of capital or capital stock or certificates of interest, except partnerships, which is organized to carry on business for its own profit or that of its members.

Section 5

(a)(1) Unfair methods of competition in or affecting commerce, and unfair or deceptive acts or practices in or affecting commerce, are hereby declared unlawful.

McCarran-Ferguson Act

Section 1012. Regulation by State law; Federal Law relating specifically to insurance; applicability of certain Federal laws after June 30, 1948

(a) The business of insurance, and every person engaged therein, shall be subject to the laws of the several States which relate to the regulation or taxation of such business.

(b) No Act of Congress shall be construed to invalidate, impair, or supersede any law enacted by any State for the purpose of regulating the business of insurance, or which imposes a fee or tax upon such business, unless such Act specifically relates to the business of insurance: *Provided*, That after June 30, 1948, the Act of July 2, 1890, as amended, known as the Sherman Act, and the Act of October 15,1914, as amended, known as the Clayton Act, and the Act of September 26, 1914, known as the Federal Trade Comission Act, as amended, shall be applicable to the business of insurance to the extent that such business is not regulated by State law.

Section 1013

(b) Nothing contained in this chapter shall render the said Sherman Act inapplicable to any agreement to boycott, coerce, or intimidate, or act of boycott, coercion, or intimidation.

APPENDIX III

Federal Antitrust Action Against State Boards

United States v. Texas State Board of Accountancy, 464 F. Supp. 400 (W.D. Tex. 1978), *aff'd*, 582 F. 2d 919 (5th Cir. 1979).

United States v. Mississippi State Board for Professional Engineers and Land Surveyors, Trade Reg. Rep. para. 45,080 (D.C. Miss. Civ. No. J-80-0235).

United States v. Alaska Board of Registration for Architects, Engineers and Land Surveyors, Trade Cas. (CCH) para. 50,837 (D. Alaska 1983).

United States v. Louisiana Board of Certified Public Accountants, Civ. No. 83-1947 (E.D. La. - filed April 15, 1983).

F.T.C. v. Rhode Island Board of Accountancy, 3 Trade Cas. (CCH) para. 22,169 (Dkt. No. 9181 - filed 1981).

F.T.C. v. Louisiana State Board of Dentistry, 3 Trade Cas. (CCH) para. 22,169 (Dkt. No. 9188 - Complaint filed October 12, 1984) (proposed consent decree - June 3, 1985).

APPENDIX IV
Federal Enforcement Actions (Professions Generally): United States Department of Justice

U.S. v. Assn. of Engineering Geologists

Complaint challenging advertising, price competition and solicitation provisions of Code of Ethics. 1985-1 Trade Cas. (CCH) para. 66,349 (C.D. Cal. 1985) (consent decree).

U.S. v. National Medical Enterprises, and NME Hospitals, Inc.

Complaint challenging the acquisition of Modesto City Hospital of Modesto by National Medical Enterprises.

U.S. v. North Dakota Hospital Assn., et al.

Complaint alleging a conspiracy by the defendant hospital association and fourteen operators of hospitals to reduce or eliminate price and other forms of competition by jointly refusing, in contract negotiations with the Department of Health and Human Services Indian Health Service Bureau, to discount the level of charges billed to the Indian Health Services Bureau for medical and surgical service and products provided to American Indians.

U.S. v. State Board of Certified Public Accountants of Louisiana

Complaint charging restriction in the sale of CPA services by adoption and enforcement of rules of professional conduct unreasonably restricting advertising and solicitation.

U.S. v. Alaska Board of Registration for Architects, Engineers and Land Surveyors

Complaint charging restriction of price competition among architects, engineers and land surveyors for their services by adoption of a rule of professional conduct prohibiting competitive bidding. CCH Trade Cas. para. 50,837 (D. Alaska 1984) (consent decree).

U.S. v. Society of Author's Representatives

Complaint charging a conspiracy to fix commissions and other fees and to restrain advertising and solicitation of clients by the Society's members. 1982-83 Trade Cas. (CCH) para. 65,210 (S.D.N.Y. 1982) (consent decree).

U.S. v. Geneva County Bar Assn.

Complaint charging a conspiracy to restrict competition for lawyers' services through the formulation, publication dissemination, and utilization of a fee schedule. 1982-1 Trade Cas. (CCH) para. 64,699 (M.D. Ala. 1982) (consent decree).

U.S. v. Coffee County Bar Assn.

Complaint charging a conspiracy to restrain trade in residential real estate closings by refusal to provide necessary legal support services to Coffee County Abstract and Title Co. and real estate agenies, and by adoption and publication of a resolution stating that provision of real estate closing services by Coffee County Abstract and Title Co. and by real estate agencies was the unauthorized practice of law.

U.S. v. McAliley, Carmichael, Dowling, Haigh, Jordan, McLean and Young

Complaint alleging a conspiracy to restrain competition for lawyers' services through the formulation, publication and dissemination of a fee schedule. 1982-2 Trade Cas. (CCH) para. 64,938 (M.D. Ala. 1982) (consent decree).

U.S. v. Cassady, Fuller & Marsh, Dowling & Carmichael; Pittman, Whittaker & Hooks; Rowe, Rowe & Sawyer; and S. Mark Jordan

Complaint alleging an agreement to raise fees charged for real estate closings. 1982-83 Trade Cas. (CCH) para. 65,122 (M.D. Ala. 1982) (consent decree).

U.S. v. New York County Lawyers Assn.

Complaint charging a conspiracy to restrict the sale of trust and estate services by corporate fiduciaries through an agreement with the Corporate Fiduciaries Assn. of New York City outlining activities of fiduciaries and of attorneys in providing trust and estate services. 1981-2 Trade Cas. (CCH) para. 64,371 (S.D.N.Y. 1981) (consent decree).

U.S. v. Hospital Affiliates International, Inc. and American Health Services, Inc.

Complaint challenging the acquisition of AHS by HAI in the provision of in-patient psychiatric and general acute-care hospitals. 1980-81 Trade Cas. (CCH) para. 63,721 (E.D. La. 1980) (preliminary injunction). 1982-1 Trade Cas. (CCH) para. 64,696 (E.D. La. 1982) (consent decree).

U.S. v. Title Insurance Rating Bureau of Arizona, Inc.

Complaint charging a conspiracy to fix prices of escrow services through agreement on and adoption and filing of schedules of escrow service rates along with a resolution to apply the schedules, and through the exchange of past, present and potential prices for escrow services. 517 F. Supp. 1053 (D. Ariz. 1981) (exemption denied); 1982-1 Trade Cas. (CCH) para. 64,483 (D. Ariz. 1982) (final judgment); 1983-1 Trade Cas. (CCH) para. 65,261 (9th Cir. 1983) (judgment affirmed).

U.S. v. American Consulting Engineers Council

Complaint alleging conspiracy to restrict the sale of engineering and land surveying services by adopting, and by members agreeing to abide by, provisions in its code of ethics and professional conduct guidelines which prohibited members from: entering competitions for engineering designs without reasonable compensation; performing services for free except for civic, charitable or religious organizations; and providing services on a contingent fee basis. 1982-2 Trade Cas. (CCH) para. 64,787 (D.D.C. 1982) (consent decree).

U.S. v. Montana Home Assn., Inc.

Complaint alleging a conspiracy to raise price for nursing home services paid under Medicaid by jointly refusing to enter into Medicaid contracts with the state except on terms agreed on by the association and by acting as the bargaining agent for nursing homes in negotiating Medicaid contracts with the state. 1982-2 Trade Cas. (CCH) para. 64,852 (D. Mont. 1982) (consent decree).

U.S. v. Mississippi State Board of Registration for Professional Engineers and Land Surveyors

Complaint charging defendant with a conspiracy to raise the price of nursing homes services paid under Medicaid by refusing to enter into Medicaid contracts with the state except on terms agreed on by the association and its members. 1980-2 Trade Cas. (CCH) para. 63,316 (D.S.C. 1980) (consent decree).

U.S. v. Allen County Indiana Bar Assn., Inc.

Complaint alleging defendant conspired to monopolize and restrain trade in the title certification business by adopting, promoting and disseminating a resolution and statement of principles to restrict the sale of title insurance without a lawyer's examination of title abstracts. 1980-81 Trade Cas. (CCH) para. 63,595 (D. Ind. 1980) (consent decree).

U.S. v. Midlands Chapter of Registered Land Surveyors, et al.

Indictment charging an unincorporated trade association and three firms of surveyors with price fixing by adopting a schedule of minimum fees. Settled by pleas.

U.S. v. Halifax Hospital Medical Center and Volusia County

Complaint alleging defendants conspired to prevent an HMO from delivering health care services by establishing a committee to discourage non-local physicians from affiliating with the HMO, by excluding participating physicians from hospital staff appointments, and by adopting and distributing a resolution opposing the HMO. 1981-1 Trade Cas. (CCH) para. 64,151 (M.D. Fla. 1981) (consent decree).

U.S. v. Illinois Podiatry Society, Inc.

Complaint charging the defendant society with restricting fee competition through the adoption, publication and circulation of relative value guides. 1977-2 Trade Cas. (CCH) para. 61,767 (D. Ill. 1977) (consent decree).

U.S. v. Texas State Board of Public Accountancy

Complaint alleging conspiracy to restrict price competition among accountants practicing in Texas by adopting, policing and enforcing a rule, approved by the state's public accounting permit holders, prohibiting competitive bidding. 464 F. Supp. 400 (D. Tex. 1978), *judgment aff'd in part, modified in part*, 592 F. 2d 919 (5th Cir.), *cert. denied*, 444 U.S. 925 (1979).

U.S. v. American Bar Assn.

Complaint charging the defendant with conspiring to unreasonably prohibit lawyers from advertising price, availability and other aspects of legal services through the adoption, publication and distribution of a provision in its code of professional responsibility prohibiting such advertisements. (Complaint dismissed).

U.S. v. American Pharmaceutical Assn. and Michigan State Pharmaceutical Assn.

Complaint charging the defendant associations with conspiring to prohibit the advertising of retail prices of prescription drugs by association members through the adoption, publication, and distribution of such a provision in their codes of ethics. 1981-2 Trade Cas. (CCH) para. 64,168 (W.D. Mich. 1981) (consent decree).

U.S. v. Alameda County Veterinary Medical Assn.

Complaint alleging agreement to adopt minimum guidelines and suggested fee schedules for veterinary services. 1977-2 Trade Cas. (CCH) para. 61,738 (D. Cal. 1977) (consent decree).

U.S. v. San Diego County Veterinary Medical Assn.

Complaint alleging agreement to adopt minimum guidelines and suggested fee schedules for veterinary services. 1976-2 Trade Cas. (CCH) para. 61,131 (D. Cal. 1976) (complaint dismissed as moot).

U.S. v. The American Society of Anesthesiologists, Inc.

Complaint alleging restriction of fee competition by the association through the promulgation, publication and dissemination of relative value guides. 473 F. Supp. 147 (S.D.N.Y. 1979) (guides upheld).

U.S. v. Oregon State Bar

Complaint charging defendant with eliminating price competition among lawyers in the sale of legal services by adopting, publishing, disseminating and utilizing uniform minimum and suggested fee schedules. 385 F. Supp. 507 (D. Ore. 1974) (summary judgment denied) (case later dismissed as moot).

U.S. v. National Society of Professional Engineers

Complaint charging defendant with eliminating price competition among its members in the sale of engineering services by adopting and enforcing a provision in its professional code of ethics prohibiting competitive bidding. 435 U.S. 697 (1978); 1978-2 Trade Cas. (subsequent final judgment). (CCH) para. 62,226 (D.D.C. 1978).

U.S. v. American Institute of Certified Public Accountants, Inc.

Complaint charging defendant with eliminating price competition among its members in the sale of accounting services by adopting and enforcing a provision in its Code of Professional Ethics prohibiting competitive bidding. 1972 Trade Cas. (CCH) para. 74,007 (D.D.C. 1972) (consent decree).

U.S. v. American Institute of Architects

Complaint charging defendant with eliminating price competition among its members in the sale of architectural services by adopting and enforcing a provision in its standards of ethical practice prohibiting competitive bidding. 1972 Trade Cas. (CCH) para. 73,981 (D.D.C. 1972) (consent decree), modified, 1972 Trade Cas. (CCH) para. 74,074 (D.D.C. 1972).

U.S. v. American Society of Civil Engineers

Complaint charging defendent with eliminating price competition among its members in the sale of engineering services through adoption and enforcement of a provision in its code of ethics prohibiting price quotations. 1972 Trade Cas. (CCH) para. 73,950 (S.D.N.Y. 1972); motion to hold defendant in civil contempt for violating 1972 decree granted, 446 F. Supp. 803 (S.D.N.Y) 1977).

U.S. v. National Funeral Directors Assn. of the United States

Complaint charging defendant association with conspiracy to prevent undertakers from advertising prices for funerals. 1968 Trade Cas. (CCH) para. 72,529 (D. Wis. 1968) (consent judgment).

U.S. v. The College of American Pathologists

Complaint alleging agreement by defendant association to fix prices for commercial laboratory services, to boycott any commercial medical laboratory not operated solely for the profit of pathologists, and to refuse positions with any profit-making hospital unless its entire medical laboratory profit was directed to a pathologist. 1969 Trade Cas. (CCH) para. 72,825 (D. Ill. 1969) (consent decree).

U.S. v. Cincinnati Insurance Board

Complaint alleging the defendant trade association through its members boycotted mutual insurance companies and other insurance companies represented by non-Board member agencies. 1963 Trade Cas. (CCH) para. 70,945 (D. Ohio 1963) (consent judgement).

U.S. v. Nassau-Suffolk Pharmaceutical Society, Inc.

Complaint alleging conspiracy to stabilize prices for drug products and related good through adherence to fair trade prices. 1963 Trade Cas. (CCH) para. 70,937 (E.D.N.Y. 1963) (consent judgment).

U.S. v. Nassau-Suffolk Pharmaceutical Society, Inc.

Complaint alleging conspiracy to fix prices of prescription drugs by issuing a price list and by urging the society's members to adhere to it. 1963 Trade Cas. (CCH) para. 70,936 (S.D.N.Y. 1963) (consent judgment).

U.S. v. Assn. of Casualty and Surety Companies, et al.

Complaint charging the Association of Casualty and Surety Companies, American Mutual Insurance Alliance and National Association of Mutual Casualty Companies with conspiring to depress and control automobile damage repair costs through the "Independent Appraisal Plan." 1963 Trade Cas. (CCH) para. 70,917 (S.D.N.Y. 1963) (consent judgment).

U.S. v. Chicago Title and Trust Co. and Kansas City Title Insurance Co.

Complaint seeking divestiture of the Kansas City Title Insurance Company from the Chicago Title and Trust Co. *Exemption denied*, 242 F. Supp. 56 (D.C. Ill. 1965); *appeal dismissed*, 385 U.S. 1022 (1967); consent judgment entered 5/23/66.

U.S. v. Utah Pharmaceutical Assn.

Complaint alleging the defendant conspired to fix prices for prescription drugs. 201 F. Supp. 29 (D. Utah 1962) (judgment against defendant).

U.S. v. Idaho State Pharmaceutical Assn.

Complaint alleging the defendant conspired to fix prices for prescription drugs. 1963 Trade Cas. (CCH) para. 70,689 (D. Idaho 1963) (consent judgment).

U.S. v. Northern California Pharmaceutical Assn., et al.

Civil complaint alleging an agreement to adopt, publish, and distribute a price schedule for prescription drugs and to induce the association's members to adhere to it. 1963 Trade Cas. (CCH) para. 70,690 (D. Cal. 1963) (consent judgment); 235 F. Supp. 378 (D. Cal. 1964) (modification denied).

U.S. v. Northern California Pharmaceutical Assn., et al.

Indictment against the Northern California Pharmaceutical Association and the chairman of its pricing committee charging an agreement to adopt, publish, and distribute a price schedule for prescription drugs and to induce the association's members to adhere to it. Defendants convicted. *Affirmed*, 306 F. 2d 379 (9th Cir.), *cert. denied,* 371 U.S. 862 (1962).

U.S. v. Arizona Pharmaceutical Assn., et al.

Complaint against the Arizona Pharmaceutical Assn., the Maricopa County Pharmaceutical Assn. and the Tucson Pharmaceutical Assn. alleging an agreement to establish and maintain a price schedule for prescription drugs and to induce Arizona pharmacists to use it. 1963 Trade Cas. (CCH) para. 70,614 (D. Ariz. 1963) (consent judgment).

U.S. v. New Orleans Insurance Exchange

Complaint alleging restraint in the sale of insurance through association bylaws requiring members to boycott all nonmember insurance agencies, mutual insurance companies, and any insurance company not using Exchange outlets or members exclusively. 355 U.S. 22 (1957).

U.S. v. Insurance Board of Cleveland

Complaint alleging defendant conspired to prevent the sale of insurance by any outlets other than through boards agents and by any methods, terms or conditions not approved by the board. 188 F. Supp. 949 (D. Ohio 1960).

U.S. v. Oregon State Medical Society, et al.

Complaint against one corporation, nine unincorporated associations, and eight individuals alleging unlawful monopolization, contracts, and conspiracies in the selling and furnishing of prepaid medical care. 343 U.S. 326 (1952) (judgment for defendant).

U.S. v. American Medical Assn., et al.

Indictment of AMA, the Medical Society of the District of Columbia, the Harris County Medical Society of Houston, Texas, the Washington Academy of Surgery and twenty-one officials of the AMA and the Medical Society of the District of Columbia (filed December 20, 1938) charging a combination and conspiracy to obstruct the operations of Group Health Association, Inc., in providing medical care and hospitalization by a group practice on a risk-sharing basis. The AMA and the Medical Society of the District of Columbia were convicted. Four defendants received a directed verdict of not guilty and the remainder were acquitted. 110 F.2d 703 (D.C. Cir. 1940); *judgment of conviction aff'd*, 130 F.2d 233 (D.C. Cir. 1942), *aff'd*, 317 U.S. 519 (1943).

APPENDIX V

Selected FTC Antitrust Actions in Health Care Services

Restraints on Advertising

Lousiana State Board of Dentistry, Dkt. No. 9188 (1985) (consent decree)

American Medical Association, 94 F.T.C. 701 (1979), *aff'd*, 638 F.2d 443 (2d Cir. 1980), *aff'd mem. by an equally divided court*, 455 U.S. 676 (1982)

American Dental Association, 100 F.T.C. 448 (1982) (consent order)

Michigan Association of Osteopathic Physicians and Surgeons, 102 F.T.C. 1092 (1983) (consent order)

Broward Medical Association, 99 F.T.C. 622 (1982) (consent order)

Washington, D.C. Dermatologic Society, 102 F.T.C. 1292 (1983) (consent order)

American Academy of Opthalmology, 101 F.T.C. 1012 (1983) (advisory opinion)

Association of Independent Dentists, 100 F.T.C. 518 (1982) (consent order)

American Optometric Assn. v. F.T.C., 626 F.2d 896 (1980)

Restraints on HMOs and Other Forms of Contract Practice

American Medical Association, 94 F.T.C. 701 (1979), *aff'd*, 638 F.2d 443 (2d Cir. 1980), *aff'd mem. by an equally divided court*, 455 U.S. 676 (1982), *order modified*, 99 F.T.C. 770 (1982) and 100 F.T.C. 572 (1982)

Forbes Health System Medical Staff, 94 F.T.C. 1042 (1979) (consent order)

American Society of Anesthesiologists, Inc., 93 F.T.C. 101 (1979) (consent order)

Medical Service Corp. of Spokane County, 88 F.T.C. 906 (1976) (consent order)

Anticompetitive Hospital Mergers

American Medical International, Inc., Dkt. No. 9153 (1984) (divestiture ordered by Commission)

Hospital Corporation of America, Inc., Dkt. No. 9161 (1984) (initial decision)

Boycotts of Cost-containment by Third-party Payors

Michigan State Medical Society, 101 F.T.C. 191 (1983)

Indiana Federation of Dentists, 101 F.T.C. 57 (1983), *rev'd*, 745 F.2d 1124 (7th Cir. 1983), *petition for cert. filed*, No. 84-1809 (U.S. May 17, 1985)

Texas Dental Association, 100 F.T.C. 536 (1982) (consent order)

Association of Independent Dentists, 100 F.T.C. 518 (1982) (consent order)

California Medical Association, 93 F.T.C. 519 (1979)

Indiana Dental Association, 93 F.T.C. 392 (1979) (consent order)

Restraints against Allied Health Practitioners

State Volunteer Mutual Insurance Co., 102 F.T.C. 1232 (1983) (consent order)

Enforcement Policy Statement Regarding Physician Agreements to Control Prepayment Plans (1981)

Hospital Privileges, including Exclusive Contracts

Burnham Hospital, 101 F.T.C. 991 (1983) (advisory opinion)

Forbes Health System Medical Staff, 94 F.T.C. 1042 (1979) (consent order)

Hope, et. al., 98 F.T.C. 58 (1981) (consent order)

Pricing Activity, including PPOs

American Society of Internal Medicine, April 19, 1985 (advisory opinion)

Health Care Management Associates, 101 F.T.C. 1014 (1983) (advisory opinion)

Enforcement Policy Statement Rearding Physicians' Agreements to Control Prepayment Plans (Sept. 25, 1981)

Association of Independent Dentists, 100 F.T.C. 518 (1982) (consent order)

California Medical Association, 93 F.T.C. 519 (1979) (consent order)

Minnesota State Medical Society, 90 F.T.C. 337 (1977) (consent order)

American College of Radiology, 89 F.T.C. 144 (1977) (consent order)

American Academy of Orthopaedic Surgeons, 88 F.T.C. 968 (1976) (consent order)

American College of Obstetricians and Gynecologists, 88 F.T.C. 955 (1976) (consent order)

Ethics and Peer Review

American Medical Association, 94 F.T.C. 701 (1979), *aff'd*, 638 F.2d 443 (2d Cir. 1980), *aff'd mem. by an equally divided court*, 455 U.S. 676 (1982)

American Academy of Ophthalmology, 101 F.T.C. 1018 (1983) (advisory opinion)

American Podiatry Association (1983) (FTC staff advisory opinion)

Rhode Island Professional Standards Review Organization, 101 F.T.C. 1010 (1983) (advisory opinion)

Iowa Dental Association, 99 F.T.C. 648 (1982) (advisory opinion)

Restraints on Other Commercial Practices

Oklahoma Optometric Association, Dkt. No. 9191 (1985) (Complaint issued)

APPENDIX VI
Antitrust Review (State of Maryland)

Attorney General's Review of Antitrust Implications
of the Powers and Conduct of Maryland's
Occupational Licensing and Regulatory Boards

Stephen H. Sachs
Attorney General

Report on the Maryland State Board of Public Accountancy

Charles O. Monk II
Assistant Attorney General
Chief, Antitrust Division

Alan M. Barr
Assistant Attorney General
The Munsey Building
Seven North Calvert Street
Baltimore, Maryland 21201

Dated: August 30, 1982

Preface

In an effort to counsel the licensing and regulatory boards of this State regarding recent developments in antitrust law, the Antitrust Division is reviewing the rules and regulations of each State board and commission. This review is necessitated by the increased scrutiny imposed upon state regulatory agencies by recent antitrust cases in which long-existing and previously accepted regulatory practices have been invalidated.

We believe this review important for several reasons. First, the public is entitled to a State government which fully complies with the requirements of the law. Second, because of the very real possibility of antitrust damage liability for State regulatory board members, it is imperative that each board's regulations and administrative practices be studied in order to protect its members.

This memorandum will summarize our review of the regulations and practices of the Maryland State Board of Public Accountancy. It will discuss our recommendations as to changes in those regulations and practices which affect competition.

A. **Summary of Review**

For purposes of this review, we looked to several sources of information, including:

1) Md. Ann. Code art. 75A, sections 1-23A (1980 Repl. Vol.), which provides the Board's statutory authority;
2) Md. Ann. Code art. 41, sections 244-256 (1980 Repl. Vol.), the Maryland Administrative Procedure Act;
3) COMAR sections 09.24.01 - .03, which contain the regulations promulgated by the Board;
4) The minutes of the Board meetings from 1977 through 1981;
5) Selected files; and
6) Conversations with the Executive Director and Assistant Director of the Board.

B. **Summary of Antitrust Analysis**

The Maryland Antitrust Act, Md. Com. Law Code Ann. sections 11-201—11-213 (1975), establishes the policy of the State favoring free enterprise and open competition. Where competitors agree to practices which unreasonably restrain competition, serious antitrust concerns are raised. *See National Society of Professional Engineers v. United States*, 435 U.S. 679 (1978). It is frequently the case that the majority of members of state regulatory and licensing boards are themselves competitors of the people they regulate. For example, three of the five members of the Maryland State Board of Public Accountancy are practicing certified public accountants ("CPAs"). Another member, a professor of accounting, is also a certified public accountant. Thus, even though Md. Ann. Code art. 75A, section 1 requires that the Board have these representatives from the profession, there is some danger that Board members may be violating the antitrust laws when they impose regulations which are outside their authority and which unreasonably restrain trade. *Cf.American Society of Mechanical Engineers, Inc. v. Hydrolevel Corp.*, 102 S. Ct. 1935 (1982).

State regulatory agencies may be exempt from the antitrust laws under a theory called the state action immunity doctrine. The Supreme Court has indicated in recent decisions that state regulatory agencies are not, by virtue of their status alone, immune from the antitrust laws. *See, e.g.,*

Goldfarb v. Virginia State Bar, 421 U.S. 773 (1975). Unless there is clear statutory authority for the competition-restricting policies of a state licensing board, the general rule favoring competition may not be supplanted by competition-restraining regulations or practices.

In *California Retail Liquor Dealers Association v. Midcal Aluminum, Inc.*, 100 S.Ct. 937 (1980), the Supreme Court set out two standards which must be met for state action immunity to attach to a regulatory program. The restraint must be both in furtherance of a "clearly articulated and affirmatively expressed" state policy and actively supervised by the State. (100 S. Ct. at 943). As to the California regulatory scheme in question, the Court stated, '[t]he national policy in favor of competition cannot be thwarted by casting such a gauzy cloak of state involvement over what is essentially a private price fixing arrangement." 100 S. Ct. at 943-44. *See also Community Communications, Inc. v. City of Boulder, Colorado*, 102 S.Ct. 835 (1982). The Maryland Court of Appeals recently applied these standards in an antitrust challenge to the Comptroller's enforcement of the Unfair Cigarette Sales Act. *Cochran v. Comptroller*, 292 Md. 3 (1981).

The initial inquiry in each case is whether there is a clear state policy to restrict competition as contrasted to vague, broad statutory mandates. Such policy must be manifested in express statutory authority. If such policy is extant, the inquiry turns to whether there is some active state supervision of the competition-inhibiting activity. Where there is a clearly expressed legislative policy and where the board affirmatively regulates within its authority to achieve the legislative objective in the least restrictive manner, it will be exempt from the antitrust laws. Where, however, there is no clearly stated legislative objective or where the agency exceeds its statutory authority, it will not enjoy state action immunity.

In *United States v. Texas Board of Public Accountancy*, 464 F. Supp. 400 (W.D. Tex. 1978), *aff'd*, 592 F.2d 919 (5th Cir.), *cert. denied*, I00 S.Ct. 262 (1979), for example, the court held that the State board did not act with state action immunity when it promulgated a rule prohibiting public accountants from making competitive bids for professional services. The board's enabling statute did not express an anticompetitive policy which would mandate such a rule. Promulgation of the rule was found to be an agreement among competitors which unreasonably restrained trade and, thus, violated the antitrust laws. Recently, the U.S. Department of Justice threatened suit against the West Virginia Accounting Board over regulations which restrained trade by limiting advertising without requisite authority. A lawsuit was avoided only when the Board agreed to amend its regulations.

In short, members of a licensing board who are members of the industry they regulate may be considered participants in a conspiracy to restrain trade if they exceed their statutory authority and, as a result, may be personally liable under the antitrust laws. *See Federal Prescription Service v. American Pharmaceutical Ass'n.*, 484 F. Supp. 1195 (D.D.C. 1980) *rev'd on other grounds*, [1981-82] Trade Reg. Rep. (CCH) para. 64,217 (D.C. Cir. 1981). However, with proper counseling and a careful analysis of the board's statutory authority and the procedures utilized by the board, personal antitrust liability may be avoided.

C. Statutory Authority

The Maryland State Board of Public Accountancy is given its grant of authority in Md. Ann. Code art. 75A, sections 1-23A (1980 Repl. Vol.). The Board is empowered generally in section 1(d) to adopt "regulations for the orderly conduct of its affairs and for the administration of this article." In addition, section 1(d) provides, "[t]he Board shall promulgate and may amend rules of professional conduct appropriate to establish and maintain a high standard of integrity and dignity in the profession of public accounting."

The statute requires anyone desiring to use the title "certified public accountant" to first obtain a certificate from the Board. Section 14.[1] It is a misdemeanor for any person to use the title "certified public accountant" without first obtaining this certificate. Section 16.

The Board is authorized to prescribe educational requirements that must be met by prospective CPAs. Section 3. The Board is also empowered to determine the form and content of the examination that people desiring to use the title "certified public accountant" must pass in order to obtain their certificate. Section 5 empowers the Board, in its discretion, to grant a reciprocal license to people who are recognized as CPAs in other states without requiring them to take an examination in Maryland. In addition, the Board is empowered to adopt continuing education requirements with which certified public accountants must comply in order to retain their certification.

The Board is authorized, after a hearing, to refuse to issue an initial certificate, or to revoke or suspend an existing certificate, of a person who is guilty of enumerated offenses, including dishonesty, fraud or gross negligence in the practice of public accountancy, conviction of a felony involving dishonesty or fraud, or violation of a rule of professional conduct promulgated by the Board under the authority granted it by article 75A. Section 12.

D. Review of Regulations and Practices

The enabling statute provides for certification and regulation of certified public accountants. The Board's regulations and enforcement activities that conform to this statutory scheme will be exempt from the antitrust laws. The vast majority of the existing regulations are within the protection of the state action immunity doctrine. To the extent, however, that the Board issues regulations which impose anticompetitive restrictions on licensees in excess of those expressly authorized by statute, it could be subject to the antitrust laws. Several of the Board's regulations do go beyond the scope of its enabling statute. This section will focus on those provisions.

1. **Advertising and Solicitation**

In COMAR section 09.24.01.04D(3), the Board has imposed substantial restrictions on the ability of CPAs to advertise their services. This regulation provides:

(3) Advertising. A licensee may not use or participate in the use of any form of public communication having reference to his professional services which contains a false, fraudulent, misleading, deceptive, or unfair statement or claim. A false, fraudulent, misleading, deceptive, or unfair statement or claim includes but is not limited to a statement or claim which:

(a) Contains a misrepresentation of fact,

(b) Is likely to mislead or deceive because it fails to make full disclosure of relevant facts;

(c) Contains any testimonial or laudatory statement, or other statement or implication that the licensee's professional services are of exceptional quality;

(d) Is intended or likely to create false or unjustified expectations of favorable results;

(e) Implies educational or professional attainments or licensing rec-

[1]But *see Comprehensive Accounting Service Corp. v. Board*, 284 Md. 474 (1979) (the term "accounting" does not come within this provision).

ognition not supported in fact;

(f) States or implies that the licensee has received formal recognition as a specialist in any aspect of the practice of public accountancy, if this is not the case;

(g) Represents that professional services can or will be competently performed for a stated fee when this is not the case, or makes representations with respect to fees for professional services that do not disclose all variables affecting the fees that will in fact be charged; or

(h) Contains other representations or implications that in reasonable probability will cause an ordinarily prudent person to misunderstand or be deceived.

The Board's enabling statute does not expressly authorize it to impose limitations on the ability of CPAs to advertise, a crucial competitive device. However, subsections (a), (b), (d), (e), (f), (g), and (h) of COMAR section 09.24.01.04D(3) are all intended to prevent fraud and deceit. We believe that these concerns are at the heart of the enabling statute's scheme of preserving the dignity and integrity of the profession, and, as such, do not constitute unreasonable restraints of trade. Accordingly, we believe that these subsections may remain in effect.[2]

On the other hand, subsection (c) goes beyond forbidding fraud or deception. It seeks to forbid CPAs from including "testimonial or laudatory" statements or statements that imply that the advertiser's services are of exceptional quality. Statements of quality are common, if not universal, in advertisements. They are important and, where not untrue, are legitimate devices by which businesses attract customers. Forbidding such statements substantially limits the types and formats of advertising that CPAs may employ in their efforts to compete with each other and with non-licensed entities that offer services in competition with CPAs (*e.g.*, bookkeeping and tax services). Accordingly, this subsection, which is not expressly authorized by the Board's enabling statute, should be deleted.

The Board has also promulgated restrictions on the ability of CPAs to solicit clients through direct personal communications, here called "solicitation." COMAR sec. 09.24.02.04D(4) provides:

(4) Solicitation. A licensee may not by any direct personal communication solicit an engagement to perform professional services;

(a) If the communication would violate sec. D(3) [improper advertising], above, if it were a public communication;

(b) By the use of coercion, duress, compulsion, intimidation, threats, overreaching, or vexatious or harassing conduct, or

(c) Where the engagement would be for a person or entity not already a client of the licensee, unless this person or entity has invited this communication or is seeking to secure the performance of professional services and has not yet engaged another to perform them.

As is the case with the advertising restrictions discussed above, the enabling statute does not expressly authorize the Board to restrict solicitation. Accordingly, this regulation may be outside the protection of the state action immunity doctrine and may subject the Board to antitrust liability if the restrictions imposed by this regulation are found to constitute unreasonable restraints of trade.

Subsection (a) forbids communications which would violate the advertising provisions discussed above. Accordingly, this subsection is permissible to the same extent that the advertising regulations are permissible. At the same time, to the extent that it incorporates by reference the impermissible portion of those regulations, COMAR section 09.24.01.04D (4) too is impermissible. Of course, the defect in this subsection will be cured by deleting the impermissible portion of the regulation it incorporates.

Subsection (b), which forbids the use of "coercion, duress, compulsion, intimidation, threats, overreaching, or vexatious or harassing conduct" appears merely to forbid outrageous conduct. It is unlikely that enforcement of this provision would be deemed an unreasonable restraint of trade. However, the language of this provision is sufficiently ambiguous that a danger exists that this provision could be utilized in an arbitrary and anticompetitive manner. Accordingly, although we believe this provision is permissible on its face, we caution the Board to invoke subsection (b) judiciously and only in circumstances involving clearly outrageous conduct.[3]

Subsection (c) forbids solicitation of a person not already a client of the licensee unless the prospective client invites the solicitation or is seeking a certified public accountant and has not yet retained another person to perform these services. This portion of the regulation is not expressly authorized by the Board's enabling statute and is clearly anticompetitive. Any effort to restrict solicitations to people who are already clients of a licensee obviously restricts competition. It serves to protect existing accounts of CPAs by forbidding other CPAs from soliciting people who have already engaged another accountant. In addition, it severely limits solicitation by a CPA of other prospective clients who do not currently have any ongoing relationship with the CPA. This too constitutes a severe restriction on the ability of CPAs to compete for new clients. Accordingly, this portion of COMAR section 09.24.01.04D(4) must be deleted.

2. Commissions

COMAR section 09.24.01.04A(3) provides:

A licensee may not pay a commission to obtain a client, or accept a commission for a referral to a client of products or services of others.

This regulation, which is not expressly authorized by the enabling statute, restricts competition by denying licensees access to one device by which they may acquire new clients. In addition, the prohibition against accepting a commission for referring clients to a product or service of another may resfain competition in fields other than accountancy. For example, under this regulation, a licensee could not accept a commission for referring a client to a computer service or a seller of word processing equipment.

COMAR section 09.24.01.04A(3) s intended to preserve the independence of certificate holders. The Board's intention is laudable. However, the Board does not have the requisite statutory authority to forbid this form of conduct. Accordingly, this regulation must be deleted. Alhough the blanket prohibition in COMAR section 09.24.01.04A(3) is not supported by statutory authority, the Board may promulgate regulations to prevent the acceptance of a commission without disclosure to the CPA's client. Such a regulation would, in our view, be permissible and ensure honesty and integrity in the relationship between the CPA and his client.

[2] We note that restrictions on advertising must also pass constitutional muster in order to be valid, for advertising is a form of speech and thus protected to a certain extent by the first Amendment. *Bates v. State Bar of Arizona*, 433 U.S. 350 (1977). However, in *Bates*, the Supreme Court stated that prohibitions on deceptive or misleading advertising do not constitute violations of protected First Amendment rights. *Id.* at 383.

[3] Solicitation regulations, like advertising regulations, must also pass First Amendment scrutiny. However, it appears that prohibitions of solicitation by use of intimidation and other forms of vexatious conduct will be sustained. *Ohralik v. Ohio State Bar Association*, 436 U.S. 447, 462 (1978).

3. Reciprocal Certification

COMAR section 09.24.03.01 outlines requirements that must be met by an out-of-state CPA who desires to obtain a reciprocal license to practice as a CPA in Maryland. This regulation provides:

The Board may waive the examination and grant a reciprocal certificate, upon application and payment of a fee, to a certified public accountant who: A. Meets the appropriate requirement in Article 75A, section 5(a)(1); B. Holds a valid certificate then in full force and effect from another State after having passed the Uniform CPA exam; and C. Meets the requirements of Article 75A, section 2, Annotated Code of Maryland at the time of application; and who (1) Meets the applicable educational requirements of Article 75A, section 3, Annotated Code of Maryland; (2) Has either practiced full time as a public accountant 5 out of the last 10 years immediately preceding his application; or (3) Has obtained 1 year of public accounting experience and 15 semester hours of accounting education at an accredited college or university and has passed courses in financial, tax, and auditing within the past 5 years.

Subsections A and B of this regulation are reasonable and clearly supported by statute. Subsection C, however, is written in an ambiguous manner and is subject to two interpretations; one reading is permissible and one reading may place unreasonable restraints on out-of-state CPAs desiring to obtain reciprocal licensure in Maryland. To our knowledge, the Board has not, to date, had occasion to determine which interpretation it deems applicable.

The clearly permissible reading of subsection C is to require the accountant seeking reciprocal licensure in Maryland to either satisfy the education requirements of section 2 of the Board's governing statute or demonstrate to the Board that he has sufficient work experience to merit a reciprocal license. This work qualification may be met by compliance with either subsection C(2) or subsection C(3).

The interpretation of this regulation which raises antitrust concerns relies upon the word "either" in subsection C(2). It would require candidates for reciprocal licensure to meet Maryland's educational requirements as provided in subsection C(1) *and* satisfy "either" one of the two work experience requirements set out in C(2) and C(3). This interpretation would, in essence, require candidates for reciprocal licensure not only to meet the normal educational standards for licensure, the required course of study and successful completion of the CPA examination[4], but also to meet substantial *additional* work experience requirements. Clearly, it makes reciprocal licensure more difficult and discourages out-of-state CPAs from practicing in Maryland.

This discriminatory interpretation of subsection C is not authorized by statute. In addition, this interpretation may be subject to challenge under the Equal Protection Clause of the United States Constitution. Accordingly, we recommend that the Board amend COMAR section 09.24.03.01 to comport with the legitimate interpretation of this regulation by deleting the word "either" in subsection C(2) and inserting it after the word "who" in the first phrase of subsection C.

4. Forecasts

COMAR section 09.24.01.04B(4) provides:

A licensee may not in the performance of professional services permit his name to be used in conjunction with any forecast of future transactions in a manner which may reasonably lead to the belief that the licensee vouches for the achievability of the forecast. The regulation is not expressly authorized by the Board's enabling statute. These restrictions may have an anticompetitive effect by limiting the ability of a certified public accountant to compete in one line of professional services, economic forecasting, with non-CPAs who are not restricted from vouching for the achievability of a forecast. Whatever other legal implications forecasting may have, this Board does not have the authority to impose the restrictions contained in this regulation. Accordingly, we recommend that COMAR section 09.24.01.04(B)(4) be deleted.

5. Quality Review

In the course of our review of the Board's regulations and practices, we were advised that the Board is interested in obtaining financial statements prepared by licensees for various state entities in order to perform a quality review of the work being done by licensees. In our view, the Board has no authority to undertake this review. The statutorily designated role of the Board is to preserve the "dignity and integrity" of the accounting profession. Section 1(d). Although it is authorized to assure itself of the competence of initial licensees, the Board is not authorized to institute a program of monitoring financial statements to assure itself that licensees are practicing in a "competent" manner following the initial licensure, except in the case of gross negligence, as provided in section 12. This is demonstrated in the continuing education provisions of section 3, where although the Board is empowered to adopt regulations with regard to continuing education, the General Assembly specifically provided that the Board may not require certificate holders to submit to the Board grades received in these continuing education courses or scores from examinations taken during these courses. Section 3(e)(4). In doing so, the General Assembly has expressed an intent to limit the inquisitorial powers of the Board in the area of ongoing quality control of accounting work. Accordingly, because the danger exists that these procedures could be used in an arbitrary, anticompetitive manner, we believe that the Board should not, absent express direction from the legislature, undertake this proposed course of action.

E. Summary of Conclusions and Recommendations

For the reasons discussed in this memorandum, certain of the Board regulations and activities inhibit competition in the accountancy profession and are not exempt from the antitrust laws under the state action immunity doctrine. There is thus a potential for personal antitrust liability should they continue. We note that the Board has already voted to implement recommendations (a) and (b), below, and urge the Board to implement the remaining recommendations contained in this report immediately.

(a) COMAR section 09.24.01.04(D)(3)(c), which prohibits advertising by certificate holders that "contains any testimonial or laudatory statements, or other statement or implication that the licensee's professional services are of exceptional quality," is unsupported by statutory authority. This provision, which has a clear anticompetitive effect, must be deleted.

(b) COMAR section 09.24.01.04d (4)(c) prohibits solicitation by licensees "where the engagement would be for a person or entity not already a client of the licensee, unless this person or entity has invited this communication or is seeking to secure the performance of professional services and has not yet engaged another to perform them." This regulation is not authorized by the Board's enabling statute and clearly restrains competition. Accordingly, it must be deleted.

---

[4] We are advised that the CPA examination in all states is a standardized examination prepared by a nationally known testing service.

(c) COMAR section 09.24.01.04A (3), which prohibits licensees from paying commissions to obtain clients or receiving commissions for referral of clients or products to others, restrains competition and is unauthorized by statute. This regulation should be deleted.

(d) COMAR section 09.24.03.01, which sets out the requirements that must be met by out-of-state CPAs seeking reciprocal licensure in Maryland, is ambiguous. In order to avoid an unauthorized and anticompetitive interpretation of this provision, we suggest that the word "either" be deleted from subsection C(2) and inserted behind the word "who" in the first phrase of subsection C.

(e) COMAR section 09.24.03.04B(4) provides that a licensee may not permit his name to be used in conjunction with forecasts of future transactions in a manner suggesting that the licensee vouches for the achievability of the forecast. This regulation is not authorized by statute and may inhibit competition between licensees and non-licensees who perform similar services. Accordingly, it should be deleted.

Finally, we have reviewed the Board's proposal to undertake an ongoing quality review of work being done by licensees. We found no statutory authority for the Board to undertake this review. In light of the possible anticompetitive effects that this review may produce, we suggest that the Board not go forward with this proposal unless it obtains express statutory authority from the General Assembly to do so.

APPENDIX VII
Selected State Antitrust and Competition Authorities and Attorney General Opinions

A. Selected State Court Authorities

Alcoholic Beverage Control of the Commonwealth of Kentucky v. Taylor Drug Stores, Inc., 635 S.W.2d 319 (Ky. 1982) (invalidated state liquor fair trade law as falling outside Midcal; no active state supervision of prices)

Attorney General of Texas v. Allstate Insurance Co., 1985-1 Trade Cas. (CCH) para. 66,472 (Tex. Ct. App. 1985) (insurance company not exempt from Texas Attorney General's civil investigative demand under the "business of insurance" exemption)

Bally Manufacturing Corporation v. New Jersey Casino Control Commission, 85 N.J. 325, 426 A.2d 1000 (N.J.), *appeal dismissed*, 102 S.Ct.77 (1981) (N.J. Casino control commission regulation prohibiting a casino from acquiring more than 50 percent of its slot machines from any one manufacturer is state action immune; commission is a state agency and actively supervises conduct)

Board of Regents of University of Oklahoma v. NCAA, 1977-1 Trade Cas. (CCH) para. 61,288 (Okla., 1977) (NCAA rule limiting number of coaches in league is not a per se violation or an unreasonable restraint of trade under Oklahoma law)

Cameron v. New Hanover Memorial Hospital, 293 S.E.2d 901, 58 N.C. App. 414, *appeal dismissed*, 297 S.E.2d 399, 307 N.C. 127 (N.C. 1982) (podiatrist challenge to denial of hospital staff privileges; judgment for defendants for failure to prove conspiracy)

Centeno v. Roseville Community Hosp., 167 Cal. Rptr. 183, 107 Cal. 3d 62 (Cal. Ct. App. 1979) (hospital exclusive radiology contract upheld under Rule of Reason)

Clark Oil & Refining Corp. v. Ashcroft, attorney general of Missouri, 639 S.W. 2d 594 (Mo. 1982) (Attorney General had power under state law to maintain damage suit on behalf of citizens)

State of Colorado v. Colorado Springs Board of Realtors, 1980-81 Trade Cas. (CCH) para. 63,653 (Colo. Dist. Ct. 1980) (realty board barred from adopting, publishing or enforcing any requirement not necessary to "efficient" operation of the multiple listing service)

Commonwealth of Massachusetts v. Massachusetts CRINC, 466 N.E.2d 792, 392 Mass. 79 (Mass. 1984) (corporation formed by competing beer wholesalers to perform all bottle and can collection and recyling not state action immune; activities alleged to be violations were not mandated by the state "bottle bill" collection legislation)

Desgranges Psychiatric Center v. Blue Cross/Blue Shield of Michigan, 1980-81 Trade Cas. (CCH) para. 63,576 (Mich. Cir. Ct. 1980) (moratorium by insurer on new outpatient clinics creates monopoly favoring current clinics and excluding new ones)

Derish v. San Mateo Burlingame Board of Realtors, 186 Cal Rptr. 390, 136 Cal.3d 534 (Cal. Ct. of App. 1982) (limiting to multiple listing service access to only licensed broker or agent held lawful under Rule of Reason) (Note: Compare antitrust analysis in *Glendale Board of Realtors v. Honsell*, 139 Cal. Rptr. 830, 72 Cal.3d 210 (Cal. Ct. App. 1977)

Finocchiaro, Inc. v. Nebraska Liquor Control Commission, 1984-1 Trade Cas. (CCH) para. 66,038 (Neb. 1984) (legislative price-setting held unconstitutional since it bore no relation to furtherance of the public health, safety or welfare)

Fischer, Spuhl, Herzwurm and Associates, Inc. v. Forrest T. Jones & Co., 586 S.W.2d 310 (Mo. 1979) (insurance company and brokers charged with illegally tying sales of group accident and health insurance to sales of life insurance were not state action immune)

Fisher v. City of Berkeley, 1985-1 Trade Cas. (CCH) para. 66,473 (Cal. 1984) (municipal rent control is lawful under the Rule of Reason)

George W. Cochran Co., Inc. v. Comptroller of the Treasury, 292 Md. 3, 437 A.2d 194 (Md. 1981) (state prohibition of below-cost cigarette sales is state action immune as legislatively mandated and state-monitored and enforced)

Gibson Distributing Co., Inc. v. Downtown Development Association of El Paso, 572 S.W.2d 334 (Tex.), *appeal dismissed*, 99 S.Ct. 606 (1978) (Sunday "blue laws" exempt under the state action doctrine)

Hackett v. Metropolitan General Hospital, 1985-1 Trade Cas. (CCH) para. 66,395 (Fla. 1985) (allegation that a medical physician was denied staff privileges as a urologist at an osteopathic hospital in order to insulate urologists on the staff from competition from medical doctors stated a claim under the Florida Antitrust Act)

Heir v. Degan, 1980-1 Trade Cas. (CCH) para. 63,269 (N.J. Sup. Ct. 1980) (regulations barring cooperative joint liquor advertising by dealers invalid as impermissible restraint on commercial speech)

Kroger Co. v. Kentucky Milk Marketing and Antimonopoly Commission, 1983-2 Trade Cas. (CCH) para. 65,585 (Ky. Cir. Ct. 1983) (Kentucky milk marketing pricing statute is not exempt under state action doctrine and conflicts with Sherman Act)

Lange v. The Nature Conservancy, Inc., 24 Wash. App. 416, 601 P.2d 963, (Ct. App. 1979), *cert. denied*, 449 U.S. 831 (1980) (conduct of conservation-environmental group is *Noerr* Protected)

Lewis-Westco & Company v. Alcoholic Beverage Control Appeals Board, 186 Cal. Rptr. 572, 136 Cal. 3d 829 (Cal. Ct. App. 1982) (state liquor pricing-posting statutes invalid as not meeting *Midcal* test)

Matossian v. Fahmie, 161 Cal. Rptr. 532, 101 Cal.3d 128 (Cal. Ct. App. 1980) (under *Noerr*, holders of licenses to sell alcoholic beverages may combine to protest the grant of a similar license to a competitor even if their sole aim is to prevent competition)

Michigan Association of Psychother-

apy Clinics v. Blue Cross Blue/Shield of Michigan, 325 N.W.2d 471, 118 Mich. App. 505 (Mich. Ct. App. 1982) (agreement by health insurer with 200 outpatient psychotherapy clinics restricting reimbursement to services by therapists with certain educational qualifications held lawful)

Moles v. White, 336 So.2d 427 (Fla. App. 1976) (neither the operator of a hospital nor the practice of medicine was held to be within the ambit of the Fla. Antitrust Statute's "trade or commerce")

New Jersey Optometric Ass'n v. Hillman-Kohan Eyeglasses, Inc., 160 N.J. Super. 81, 388 A.2d 1299 (Sup. Ct. N.J. 1978) (court refused to compel state optometry board to institute proceedings to halt disputed optometric practices)

New York v. Horseman's Benevolent & Protective Ass'n., 1976-2 Trade Cas. (CCH) para. 61,213 (N.Y. Sup. Ct. 1976) (owners' and trainers' association withdrawal of horses from N.Y. race tracks to protest failure to enact legislation was an illegal boycott under the Donnelly Act)

New York v. New York State Society of Opthalmic Dispensers, Inc., 1980-1 Trade Cas. (CCH) para. 63,074 (Sup.Ct. N.Y. Co. 1979) (consent decree) (association of opthalmic dispensers prohibited from refusing to deal with eyeglass lens and frame manufacturers who participate in employee-insured plans or who sell directly to covered employees)

New York v. Queensboro Farm Products, Inc., 1982-83 Trade Cas. (CCH) para. 65,071 (Sup. Ct. Queens Co. 1982) (alleged milk price-fixing and allocation of customers - not immune)

Ohio ex rel. Brown v. Alliance Dental Society, 1976-1 Trade Cas. (CCH) para. 60,944 (Ohio Ct. Common Pleas 1976) (alleged boycott of Ohio welfare patients) (final judgment)

People v. Roth, 52 N.Y.2d 440, 420 N.E.2d 929 (1980) (medical profession under New York law, not subject to antitrust prohibitions)

People of State of Colorado v. Colorado Shorthand Reporters Association, 1976-1 Trade Cas. (CCH) para. 60,685 (Colo. 1976) (consent decree) (shorthand reporters association prohibited from placing any restrictions regarding uses for services)

State of Arizona v. Prescott Board of Realtors, 1980-81 Trade Cas. (CCH) para. 63,599 (Ariz. Sup. CCt. 1980) (consent decree) (Arizona Board of Realtors barred from agreeing on real estate commission rates, methods of payment, or split arrangements)

Reinfeld, Inc. v. Schieffelin & Co., 1983-2 Trade Cas. (CCH) para. 65,669 (N.J. Sup. Ct. 1983) (order preventing wholesalers liquor regulation exempt under *Parker* doctrine since state actively supervised and was involved in effectuating law)

State of Wisconsin, ex rel State Bar of Wisconsin v. Peterson, 1979-2 Trade Cas. (CCH) para. 62,751 (Wisc. Cir. Ct. 1979) (Sherman Act counter-claim to a prosecution for unauthorized practice of law dismissed under state action doctrine)

Twilight Swimming Pool, Inc. v. Commissioner of Dept. of Conservation 1980-81 Trade Cas. (CCH) para. 63,732 (Tenn. Ct. App. 1981) (state acts in sovereign capacity in establishing swimming pools which compete with the private sector and is immune under state action doctrine)

Washington v. Tacoma-Pierce County Multiple Listing Service, et al., 1980-81 Trade Cas. (CCH) para. 63,849 (Wash. Sup. Ct. 1980) (attorney general's antitrust action against Board of Realtors for improper use of multiple listing service should not have been dismissed; state administrative agency has no primary jurisdiction and agency could not confer antitrust exemption)

Younger v. Jensen, 1980-1 Trade Cas. (CCH) para. 63,172 (Cal. Sup. Ct. 1980) (federal Natural Gas Act does not preempt state investigation into possible antitrust violations)

B. Selected Attorney General Opinions

Opinion of the Attorney General of Arizona, 1982-83 Trade Cas. (CCH) para. 65,084 (1982) (discusses immunity of "consortium" authorized by Arizona health care cost containment statute)

Opinion of the Attorney General of Arkansas, 1977-1 Trade Cas. (CCH) para. 61,349 (1977) (system of state royalties would be exempt under *Parker* doctrine)

Opinion of the Attorney General of Connecticut, 1977-2 Trade Cas. (CCH) para. 61,581 (1977) (regulation by Connecticut Architectural Registration Board prohibiting architects from submitting bids violates both federal and Connecticut antitrust law)

Opinion of the Attorney General of Iowa, 1978-1 Trade Cas. (CCH) para. 62,000 (1978) (hospital rate review program authorized by Iowa law would be lawful provided there is active state supervision)

Opinion of the Attorney General of Louisiana, 1984-1 Trade Cas. (CCH) para. 65,996 (1983) (ordinance restricting the solicitation of cable customers is not immune from antitrust challenge)

Opinion of the Attorney General of Michigan, 1978-1 Trade CAs. (CCH) para. 61,828 (1978) (discusses legality of banning advertising by professionals)

Opinion of the Attorney General of Michigan, 1982-1 Trade Cas. (CCH) para. 64,484 (1982) (volume purchases by state agency for statewide welfare program immune from antitrust challenge)

Opinion of the Attorney General of Nebraska, 1984-1 Trade Cas. (CCH) para. 65,884 (1984) (approval by Nebraska Power Review Board of agreements between power suppliers exempts the agreements under *Midcal*)

Opinion of the Attorney General of North Carolina, 1976-2 Trade Cas. (CCH) para. 61,129 (1976) (setting maximum price for hearing aids under Medicaid is not exempt from antitrust challenge since legislation does not specifically sanction such price setting)

Opinion of the Attorney General of Ohio, 1984-1 Trade Cas. (CCH) para. 65,796 (1983) (general discussion of legality of preferred provider organizations under the antitrust laws)

Opinion of the Attorney General of Oklahoma, 1976-1 Trade Cas. (CCH) para. 60,886 (1976) (minimum fee schedule established by State Board of Barber Examiners pursuant to statute immune from antitrust attack)

Opinion of the Attorney General of Oklahoma, 1980-2 Trade Cas. (CCH) para. 63,381 (1980) (exclusion of dry cleaners from laws prohibiting minimum fees by professionals does not render statutes void as a violation of equal protection)

Opinion of the Attorney General of Tennessee, 1984-1 Trade Cas. (CCH) para. 65,864 (1984) (local electrical codes do not have automatic antitrust immunity but there is no violation because the benefit to the public's health, safety and welfare from preventing fires outweighs any anticompetitive effect it might have)

Opinion of the Attorney General of Texas, 1982-2 Trade Cas, (CCH) para. 64,735 (1982) (Texas Alcohol Beverage Board could not refuse to honor a civil investigative demand from the U.S. Department of Justice, even if information sought was allegedly "confidential" when filed with the Board)

Opinion of the Attorney General of Vermont, 1979-2 Trade Cas. (CCH) para. 62,912 (1979) (rules of board of public accountancy prohibiting accountants from soliciting customers are probably unlawful and not immune since regulation not included under state authorization to regulate profession)

Opinion of the Attorney General of West Virginia, 1980-81 Trade Cas. (CCH) para. 63,676 (1980) (extensive discussion of several situations involving Medicaid providers, *Parker* and *Noerr* doctrines).